Eating Well
on a Budget

SARA LEWIS

2nd Edition
© 1993 Sara Lewis
Published by Age Concern England
1268 London Road
London SW16 4ER

Editorial Deborah Murdoch, Odile Hearn,
David Moncrieff
Design & Typesetting Eugenie Dodd
Production Marion Peat
Copy Preparation Vinnette Marshall
Printed by Grosvenor Press Limited,
Portsmouth

A catalogue record for this book is available
from the British Library.

ISBN 0–86242–120–9

Contents

Sponsor's foreword

Dear reader,

In an ideal world we could all look forward to a contented retirement without financial worries. Unhappily there are many for whom this is not the case. Pensions are often smaller than anticipated and living costs have risen considerably over the last two decades.

We are fortunate in this country in having a wide variety of fresh foods available throughout the year. To show how economically and to what good effect we can use them is the purpose of this book, which Unigate is pleased to sponsor.

Eating Well on a Budget is aimed specifically at the older reader whose slower pattern of life demands a quite different diet to that of the more active young. High energy foods become less important, whilst the need for additional calcium to control poor circulation and brittle bones becomes more so, as does a correct vitamin intake.

This book seeks to deal with these and other dietary requirements of older people.

It is all too easy when cooking for just one person, as many older people do, to feel that it is not important to eat well. We hope that this book will provide useful recipes which stimulate the cooking of tastier, healthier and cheaper meals.

Ross Buckland
Chief Executive
Unigate PLC

About the author

Sara Lewis is a cookery journalist and a qualified home economist; she has specialised in writing for practical magazines on cooking for budget conscious family meals, but is also known for her creative flair in her work for gourmet magazines. Previously cookery editor for Family Circle magazine, she recently 'retired' from full-time work to look after her family; she is the freelance cookery editor of Practical Parenting magazine.

Acknowledgments

I am particularly grateful for the wise approach to healthy eating suggested by Dr Juliet Gray BSc, PhD, SRD, Consultant Nutritionist, and for the information and advice provided by:

- The Department of Health;
- The Health Education Authority;
- The Ministry of Agriculture, Food and Fisheries;
- The Food Safety Advisory Centre;
- County Trading Standards Department, West Sussex.

My warm personal thanks go to my mother, newly retired when I began to work on this book, who has been a great source of inspiration and support.

Sara Lewis
September 1992

Author's introduction

Most people entering retirement are in the prime of life. There are usually many years ahead to plan and budget for, and the experience and wisdom of middle age provides confidence that, with the right information, this will be done effectively.

Budgeting for and planning food shopping will, of course, change considerably when a complete weekly menu is needed instead of reliance on, say, the office canteen for five meals a week. Transferring the money spent at the till there into the home food shopping purse needs careful thought.

The obvious priority is good eating. Nowadays, however, 'good' should have two senses: good tasting but also good for the health. Yet, while healthy eating is something most people have accepted in principle, they may be uncertain when it comes down to details.

Most people are prepared to spend on good healthy food once its importance has been proved, but they will still want to eat cost-effectively whatever their personal budget.

What are the healthy, delicious recipes to follow and the good foods to buy? Are there particular dietary points for those in mid-life or beyond to consider? Should all the recent food scares be taken seriously? Will eating healthily mean dull, worthy meals? Will it cost more – and take longer – shopping for special ingredients?

This book aims to answer all these questions. Although most of the information makes good sense for everybody, it is specifically presented here for those who are retiring from work and want to know how they will need to adjust. They will find facts, guidelines and advice on running a kitchen for planning and budgeting good healthy meals.

The recipes, all cost-conscious, contain further cookery tips at relevant points and form a practical demonstration of how to eat well each week.

But first of all, the preliminary chapters deal with the background information you'll need to shop in a more informed, cost-effective way in order to eat better and more healthily than ever before.

Sara Lewis

Sara Lewis

1 | Healthy eating

Why it's worthwhile

Over recent years the importance of choosing a healthy balanced diet has been stated frequently, but the habit has not yet been adopted nationally. It is worth reiterating briefly just why medical advice is so earnest about this. We are advised to try to eat healthily for two main reasons:

■ To prolong life and, specifically, to cut down the likelihood of sickness or illnesses, ranging from heart disease to food poisoning, compounded by a bad diet or caused by poor hygiene.

■ To improve the quality of life, because those accustomed to eating well feel well.

Principles

Depending on an individual's pre-retirement diet, an attempt to eat well may mean switching to different foods to a greater or lesser extent. It will certainly not mean eating dull dishes or going hungry.

Over the last few years many readers will have already made some changes in their diet, and for them this section will serve to suggest what may still need to be done. These are the basic principles to follow for a healthy diet:

■ introduce more high-fibre foods

■ cut down on fat

■ reduce consumption of sugar and salt

- eat vegetables, whether fresh or frozen, at least twice a day and several pieces of fresh fruit daily. Remember that the body cannot store vitamin C so you need to make sure your diet includes it daily.

Aim to avoid except occasionally:

- deep fried foods
- butter, full-fat milk and cream
- bought cakes, pastries and biscuits.

The basic nutritional elements needed to build and maintain a healthy body are:

- carbohydrates
- protein
- fat
- vitamins and minerals.

The importance of variety

Eating healthily may seem a burden because it can be a considerable task to discover exactly which foods are high in which nutrients, vitamins and minerals. However, this need not be the case.

Although the formula 'go for a healthy, balanced diet' is a useful one, it is easier simply to aim for plenty of variety in any one week's meals; in fact, to eat as many different basic foods as possible. Specifically, choose foods from two or three of the groups below for each meal and vary the groups over the course of the day and week.

- **Starchy foods**
  eg bread, breakfast cereals, pasta, rice and potatoes
- **Vegetables and fruit**
  eg leafy dark green vegetables such as broccoli, greens, spinach and watercress and citrus fruits
- **Meat and alternatives**
  eg lean meat and poultry, fish and fish products, eggs, beans, lentils and nuts

- **Dairy products**
  eg milk, cheese and yogurt
- **Fats and oils**
  (but sparingly).

Better balance

It is the traditional British diet which nutritionists wish to see changed. Other ethnic diets, for instance a Mediterranean diet which is based on higher consumption of vegetables and pasta and uses olive oil, do not give rise to such concern.

Everyone, however, can usefully check over the following information, based on recognising the value of fibre and the danger of too much fat in the diet. Nutritionists want us to eat more fibre and to learn where the richest sources are. They suggest we should curtail, drastically, the amounts of fatty foods consumed.

Increasing fibre

In previous centuries, there was plenty of fibre in the British diet – it was the introduction of refined and processed foods at a cheap price (white bread, sugary biscuits, sweet desserts and drinks) which brought problems.

It is only comparatively recently that it has been realised how necessary fibre is for good health. To get the amount of fibre eaten in Britain up to a satisfactory level, it is currently being said that most people need to double their consumption of fruit and vegetables.

Fibre is found in plant foods and foods with a plant origin:

- cereals
- seeds
- beans, peas
- vegetables and fruit.

There are two types of fibre, both vitally important: the type which predominates in cereals is vital to keep the bowel system working properly and so avoid constipation; the type which predominates in oats, fruit and vegetables helps correct blood cholesterol levels.

It is advisable to switch to wholemeal or Granary bread, to use wholemeal flour or a mixture of wholemeal and white flour whenever feasible when baking, and to include a variety of white and brown rice, lentils, dried or canned beans and pasta in the diet. When preparing potatoes, whether for boiling, steaming or baking, leave their skins on; base meals also on rice or pasta. Baked beans, once considered humble fare, are now seen to be a nutritious quick meal. If served on wholemeal toast, sprinkled with a little grated cheese, they form a protein-rich meal with plenty of fibre. Learn to stretch mince mixtures by adding continental green lentils or use them in main meals as an alternative to meat; they provide fibre as well as vegetable protein.

When changing over to a fibre-rich diet, it is important to ensure you take between six and eight drinks a day, as fibre absorbs fluid.

Decreasing fat

Medical opinion is that eating less fat is vital to anyone under 75 years of age, as it helps reduce the levels of cholesterol in the blood and so lessens the risk of coronary heart disease. As fat is immensely high in calories, cutting intake will also help in a programme of weight reduction if needed.

On the other hand, the aim should be to eat more oily fish, which are rich in certain polyunsaturates; these are believed to help reduce the ability of the blood to clot. This means they may help to reduce the likelihood of thrombosis and therefore heart attacks. Everyone, whatever their age, is advised to try to eat oily fish (such as mackerel, herring or salmon) at least once a week.

The main methods of reducing the amount of fat in the diet are as follows:

- Trim off visible fat from meat and switch to extra lean mince (it's more expensive, but you will find you can use less).

- Grill rather than fry whenever possible and prick sausages so that the fat can run out; drain well before eating.

- Cook joints on a roasting rack so fat drips away, and make gravy with the meat juices after pouring off the surface fat.

- Use a non-stick pan or wok for frying; you need only add a scant tablespoon or a few teaspoons of oil. Try to use as little as possible and switch to sunflower oil or olive oil for browning meat or stir-frying vegetables.

- Employ the cooking technique known as dry frying. Start cooking 'regular' mince or streaky bacon over a low heat till the fat begins to run out then increase heat to brown.

- When spreading, use all fats sparingly, whether butter, margarines rich in polyunsaturates or reduced-fat spreads.

- Keep chips or any deep-fried food for a treat; perhaps once a week, then once a fortnight. Drain them well on kitchen paper after cooking . Choose frozen oven-bake chips which are less fatty than traditional deep-fried chips.

- Switch to semi-skimmed milk, then, once used to the taste, change to skimmed. In this form, all the protein, vitamins and minerals provided by milk are still available without the fat content, although amounts of vitamins A and D are reduced.

- Use natural yogurt and skimmed milk when making sauces and puddings. Try Greek yogurt in place of double cream and reduced-calorie mayonnaise in place of traditional mayonnaise.

Just a pinch of salt

There has been much discussion by the experts about the link between large amounts of salt in the diet and high blood pressure. Although this has not been proved conclusively, medical advice is to heed the possible risk.

Start by monitoring the amount of salt added to food in cooking and reduce this gradually.

- Add a little salt when cooking so the flavour will be absorbed.

- Taste food first rather than automatically sprinkling more salt on; it may be that more is not needed. Dishes made with aromatic herbs and spices need less salt to flavour them, so experiment using more of these.

- Cut down on salty snacks; there are large quantities of salt in unexpected foods, for instance in some sweet biscuits.

- If using stock cubes or soy sauce in a recipe, far less salt or no additional salt at all may be needed as both of these contain it already.

Beat sugar

The fact that it is advisable to cut down sugar consumption is very well known. This is particularly important for those of retirement age as it is progressively easier to put on weight and much harder to lose it in later life, when the amount of activity and exercise taken generally diminishes. The calories which sugar provides are 'empty' ones. Sugar loads on weight but does not have food value.

Much of the sugar consumed each week comes as an insidious invader; it's there in many convenience foods including ones which are primarily good, from baked beans to breakfast cereals.

Always check the labels to see how high up sugar occurs (ingredients are listed in order of quantity; for more details see Chapter 4.) It is possible to avoid sugar by choosing:

- canned fruit in natural juice rather than syrup

- low-sugar, high-fibre cereals or brands of muesli without added sugar
- jam with a low sugar content which can be kept in the fridge
- unsweetened fruit juices
- low-calorie soft drinks.

Eat more fresh fruit instead of processed products and puddings. In these more health conscious days, the claim 'without added sugar' is likely to be prominently displayed.

Caution on snacks

For frail elderly people, snacks can be important if the appetite has diminished. If that is the case it is important to aim to make the small occasional meals which are planned as nutritious as possible, but genuine loss of appetite should be reported to your doctor.

For everyone else, it is advisable to avoid snacks and instead aim to eat main meals along the lines suggested in the weekly recipes. There are several health disadvantages in eating snacks: if the extra calorie intake throughout the day leads to being overweight, there will be strain on the heart. In addition, 'snacking' is likely to mean that the wish for a main meal diminishes and consequently, important nutrients will be forgone.

Bought cakes, pastries and biscuits may taste good, but they are high in sugar as well as being high in fats. If these figure in your present diet as snacks or if you enjoy them at afternoon tea or morning coffee every day it would be advisable to consider cutting them out. It might be possible to try one of the herbal or fruit teas widely on sale; with these a snack of a few mixed nuts and raisins is sustaining. Some people find it helpful to promise themselves, just once a week, a particular treat; a favourite chocolate bar or sugary cake; they take time choosing which it shall be and enjoy it all the more.

An apple, banana or low-fat yogurt, a scrubbed carrot or a slice of wholemeal bread will give you the energy you need without the harmful effect of eating a cake, biscuit or pastry.

Beware at breakfast

Breakfast should be an important meal of the day. However, the traditional British cooked breakfast of bacon and eggs is high in fat, so switch instead to the higher fibre wholegrain cereals – Shredded Wheat, Weetabix, All-Bran, muesli – and stewed prunes, dried apricots or fresh fruit. Porridge made with semi-skimmed milk is a tasty alternative. As at any time of day, opt for wholemeal bread and switch to a low-fat spread.

2 | Food scares

Should we worry?

There has been a dramatic improvement in food storage and handling over the past 40 years. This began with the widespread introduction of refrigeration prolonging the safe storage life of many foods and continued with the introduction of freezers into shops and the home. Over the years, ever higher standards of food hygiene and food production have been required. Large numbers of customers at supermarkets results in fast turnover of stock; hence supplies of fresh food are constantly delivered.

Yet at one time newspapers, radio and TV seemed to report a new warning about foods almost every week. The safety of soft cheeses, eggs, beef and pâté has been questioned, and the possibility of problems with wrapping food in cling film has been raised. Not only does food poisoning still persist, but records indicate that it is in fact on the increase.

All forms of food poisoning are preventable. While those involved in different parts of the food chain – farmer, manufacturer, distributor, and retailer bear their share of responsibility, each individual consumer can also do a great deal to prevent food poisoning by understanding what will and will not deter dangerous growth of bacteria (see Chapter 3).

Most at risk

Certain groups of people are more susceptible than others to food poisoning and food-related problems. Consult this list, issued by the Department of Health, to see if you are among those who should take special precautions:

- frail elderly people
- those who are ill or are convalescing
- those who are taking medicines which suppress their body's natural immunity to infection
- those on extensive treatment with antibiotics or those receiving chemotherapy
- those with reduced ability to fight infection, whether they are diabetics or transplant patients or AIDS sufferers, or whether they are alcoholics or drug abusers.

The major dangers

Salmonella

Salmonella bacteria are one of the most common causes of food poisoning. Symptoms vary from abdominal pain to fever, diarrhoea and sometimes vomiting – these usually begin 12–36 hours after eating contaminated food. Illness usually lasts two to three days. It is possible to be a carrier even after the symptoms have disappeared. So on hearing that others have become ill after a meal taken together, contact your doctor for advice.

Most cases of this type of food poisoning can be traced to uncooked or badly cooked foods or food that has been cooked and then contaminated. (This could happen, for example, if cheese is cut with a knife that has been previously used for raw meat without it being thoroughly washed first.) Salmonella is particularly associated with poultry and eggs which therefore need particular care.

Salmonella bacteria are killed when food is thoroughly cooked. Consequently, when cooking or reheating it is vital that foods are heated until they are piping hot (over 70° C throughout).

This is comparatively easy in the case of poultry which is always served cooked right through. But a difficulty arises in the case of eggs, which are often lightly cooked, as in scrambled egg, or not cooked at all, as in chocolate mousse.

Hard boiled eggs can be considered safe for everyone provided they have been bought, stored and prepared properly (see below). Softly cooked eggs should be avoided by anyone in the Department of Health's 'at risk' categories unless you use pasteurised eggs (available in liquid or dried form from most supermarkets). It is advisable for everyone to avoid those rare recipes using raw eggs where no pasteurised substitute is possible (eg steak tartare).

Follow these guidelines to cut out a significant proportion of salmonella risk when buying and storing eggs.

- Always buy eggs from a reputable supplier with a quick turnover.

- Never buy or use cracked eggs.

- Check use-by dates before purchasing (see also Chapter 4: 'How labels help').

- Store eggs in their box in the fridge away from other raw foods, particularly raw meat.

- Use within two weeks of purchase.

- Always store egg dishes in the fridge (except unfilled meringues or sponge cakes which can be stored in an airtight container).

Listeria

There is only a very small risk of a healthy person contracting listeriosis, which is caused by the bacteria *listeria monocytogenes* and which, in its mild form, resembles influenza. It is less of a concern to those in middle age and beyond, for the greatest risk is to pregnant mothers as it can cause miscarriage, stillbirth, or severe illness in a new-born baby.

However, while good kitchen practices (see Chapter 3) will keep infections to a minimum, listeria bacteria do pose a risk because they can continue to multiply at fridge temperature. It is wise for anyone on the 'at risk' list to avoid all foods which have been found to contain high levels of listeria bacteria.

These are:		Choose instead:
■ raw unpasteurised milk	⟶	pasteurised, sterilised and UHT milk
■ soft mould-ripened cheese, eg Brie, Camembert, Danish blue	⟶	hard cheeses, processed soft cheeses, cheese spreads and yogurt
■ pre-cooked chiller meals and roasted poultry	⟶	frozen meals
■ meat, fish or vegetable pâté	⟶	canned pâté and jars of meat or fish paste, fermented and dehydrated meats, eg salami
■ soft whip ice cream from machines.	⟶	block ice cream.

BSE

Bovine spongiform encephalitis is a newly discovered disease – identified as recently as 1986. It affects the brain and central nervous system of adult cattle. BSE is very like the disease scrapie which has long been known to affect sheep. The cause of BSE is thought to be the practice of feeding cattle with meat and bone meal derived from infected sheep.

The Government has tried to stamp out any spread of BSE by:

■ banning the use of specified offals in all animal and pet foods

■ banning consumption of parts of the cattle which harbour BSE

■ slaughtering any animals that show signs of BSE.

As a result of this stringency, beef and lamb are currently said to be completely safe to eat; the situation continues to be monitored and reported on.

Misuse of cling film

A further risk to health has been perceived in the way cling film is used in direct contact with food and the possibility of it being carcinogenic. Manufacturers counter this claim, and it is not absolutely proven. What is known is that the plasticides in the cling film, or the material that makes it stretchy, can migrate into food it is touching.

However, this migration only occurs when the cling film is in direct contact with fatty foods. So the advice is not to use stretchy cling film to wrap cheese, butter, cut avocados, bacon or sausages.

It is only the stretchy types of cling film which are thought to be implicated. It is perfectly safe to opt for polythene sandwich bags instead. Cling film is safe to use with other types of food and when it is not in direct contact with food: if a container needs to be covered when microwaving, for instance.

Pesticides

The benefits to world agriculture of using pesticides are well known. As well as improving crop yields, they extend the life of produce by protecting it from pests and diseases during storage and they improve hygiene by killing flies, cockroaches and other food hazards. They guard against the impact of malaria-carrying mosquitoes as well as plagues of locusts and rodents.

The enthusiastic use of pesticides, however, has now led to anxiety, particularly over residues. The term pesticide actually covers all the following: insecticides; wood preservatives; masonry biocides; bird and animal repellants; herbicides; soil sterilants; rodenticides; fungicides; plant growth regulators and food storage protectors as well as anti-fouling paints for boats and public hygiene and industrial pest control products.

This vast proliferation of chemicals being used in the environment is not done without regulation. It would be hard to forgo the benefits all these substances bring. It is estimated that if we were prevented from using pesticides entirely, 30 per cent of world crops would be lost – and that is the figure before harvest.

Government bodies attempt to ensure that residues of pesticides are not left on our food by means of sampling, vetting and consultation on standards carried out by impartial medical practitioners. To date, maximum residue levels (MRLs) have been laid down covering meat and dairy products, cereals, fruits and vegetables, both UK grown and imported from abroad. It is an offence to leave residues above the levels laid down.

Some of the pesticides formulated before these levels were established were subsequently found to stay in the environment for long periods; indeed they are still here. The use of these on crops has been discontinued and the Government surveillance data indicate the levels are falling. The newer pesticides now in use are less persistent and it is believed that when properly used, the residual levels are low or even undetectable.

Washing

Some pesticides are not absorbed by the plant but are present on the surface. These can be reduced by careful washing or removed by peeling.

Systemic pesticides, however, enter the cells of plants and these cannot be removed. An acceptable daily intake (ADI) for each pesticide is established in order to ensure that residues of systemics will not constitute any danger. An ADI is that amount which can be consumed daily for a lifetime without appreciable risk. In establishing this, the diet of people who consume large or even extreme amounts of products which might contain residues is assessed as well as average consumers.

Maximum residue levels (MRLs) are, the Government claims, set very strictly, with the aim that the likely intake of pesticides from food bought in this country should be well within the ADI.

Organic option

If you want to avoid residues, choosing organic food, now on sale at many supermarkets as well as at specialist shops, is best. Remember, however, that although organic food is grown without deliberate application of pesticides, it may not be possible to eliminate totally some of the older, persistent residues in the environment.

Alar

There was understandable alarm felt when it was discovered that a growth regulator, Alar, was being used on apples and that it left residues which could not be removed by washing or peeling. Alar is sprayed on trees to help develop fruit of uniform size and to prevent fruit drop. It is no longer manufactured or available in this country, although the Independent Advisory Committee on Pesticides concluded there was no risk to health from Alar-sprayed fruit provided it had been used correctly. This is because they estimated adults would need to consume up to 30,000 treated apples daily and babies 400 jars of apple dessert daily to approach the acceptable daily limit and clearly this is impossible.

TECNAZENE
This is a fine, white powder used to prevent potatoes from sprouting during storage. Potatoes labelled organic will not have been treated and new potatoes are unlikely to have been dusted with tecnazene.

For nutritional value it is best to eat potatoes in their skins without peeling them. So as tecnazene has been found by researchers testing a sample of washed potatoes, it is advisable to wash maincrop potatoes well before use although there is an additional safety factor in that 80 per cent of tecnazene is destroyed by cooking.

WAX
Fruit is waxed to prevent dehydration as well as to give a 'cosmetic' glossy appearance. The wax sometimes contains a fungicide to prevent spoiling. Consumers are advised to wash all fruit before eating if the peel is going to be consumed, to remove soil and dust with their impurities. However, washing in cold water will not remove wax or any fungicide present.

If you dislike the idea of eating waxed fruits, remember that not all fruits are waxed. Those most likely to be given a coating are: apples, oranges, lemons and limes. (Unless you want to use the zest of an orange you will, of course, remove the wax when peeling the fruit.) You are unlikely to find waxed varieties of the following fruits in this country: melons, plums, pears, pineapples.

Use of wax is allowed in this country because it is considered harmless: it is usually either beeswax or wax from the leaf of the Brazilian wax palm. Ask the greengrocer or supermarket section head to direct you to unwaxed fruits if you dislike this idea, or choose organic produce which is never waxed.

Water impurity

The growth of knowledge about environmental pollution has led to anxiety about the purity of tap water. It's not always realised that water is a finite resource; constantly recycled, it has been estimated to take around 20 years to work its way through the water table. In the course of this it is liable to be contaminated by a variety of chemicals and heavy metals that are considered dangerous. Fertilisers, for instance, leach from farmland into the rivers and the water cannot then be used for public supplies.

Water companies are now spending extra sums building more sensitive filtration plants in order to meet European standards – 99.6 per cent of water supplies are now said to meet all these standards all of the time. This move towards 100 per cent compliance is reflected in increased water rates.

HOW MANY POLLUTANTS?
EC directives fix the maximum permitted level of nitrates at 50 milligrams per litre of water, 200 micrograms for aluminium and 50 micrograms per litre for lead. By law, any local water company must give details of what is in the supply, including contaminants. To enquire about your water, you can find the name of the company on your water rates bill.

The Department of the Environment considers that although nitrate levels can be particularly high in an arable area such as East Anglia, tap water there is still safe to drink. This applies even when EC levels are exceeded, though this level should not be consistently high for many years.

The new filtration plants being installed or already in use tackle the problem of pesticides in the water supply. In parallel, companies are being encouraged to reform current practice. For example Atrazine, previously employed on a large scale to keep trackside weeds under control, is no longer used by British Rail.

The individual can help by cultivating a greater awareness of the problems facing the water companies. For instance, remember that sewers are part of the water supply as a whole, since water is filtered and recycled. So it is not right (as used to be advised) to dispose of garden insecticides and fertilisers or other chemicals by pouring them down the drain; if you do so, you are adding them to the water supply.

If your house was built before 1976, check if it has lead pipes. These are now prohibited as the metal from them can enter the water supply. Water from lead pipes should be left to run for about three minutes before use as drinking water.

FILTERING CONTAMINANTS

Government scientists assure us that contaminants in tap water are at a safe level, but it is increasingly popular to remove as many as possible by using home filter systems.

These currently come in two types – the individual jug and the plumbed-in option.

A plumbed-in filter will range in price up to several hundred pounds for a type which does not need replacement cartridges. As well as the cost of the plumber initially, there will be annual running costs to consider for these types.

Much cheaper, an individual jug treats only small amounts of water, which should be stored in the refrigerator and used the same day. The basic jug is cheap but the filters, which usually need to be changed monthly, are comparatively expensive. If you want to pursue this option, choose a water filter carefully after comparing the different brands and the percentage of lead and aluminium they remove; some will filter out more than 80 per cent of pollutants, some as little as 20 per cent.

An electronic jug filter now available is more expensive than a basic jug type but removes large percentages of pollutants, including heavy metals, and 90 per cent of nitrates. It has a longer-life cartridge and will also remove the problem of limescale for those in hard water areas.

3 | Review your kitchen craft

Bacteria alert

When retirement means someone is based at home all day instead of going out to work, the kitchen inevitably gets used much more. The air temperature is likely to be warmer and the fridge will be opened more times in the day and so on. Warm conditions encourage harmful bacteria to multiply.

All fresh food contains bacteria, most of which do no harm – some, such as the bacteria in cheese, are actually beneficial. If, however, food is inadequately stored, handled or cooked, harmful bacteria can multiply and eventually cause food poisoning.

This chapter provides a checklist for the best and safest way to use the kitchen so that harmful bacteria are removed, deterred from growth or killed.

Effective cleaning

The greatest source of bacteria in a kitchen is likely to be on the human occupants, hence the importance of washing hands before and after handling food, or, obviously, after a trip to the dustbin or blowing the nose. Cover any cut or abrasion with a waterproof dressing.

Hands should be washed when changing from handling raw foods to cooked ones as there is a danger that bacteria from the raw food will be transferred.

Invest in separate chopping boards and knives to use for raw and for cooked foods and do not mix the two; ideally have another board for use when preparing fish. Polypropylene boards are easy to scrub clean; it is very difficult to remove all bacteria from wooden boards and utensils.

Keep all the kitchen work surfaces and utensils really clean by washing them with hot soapy water. In addition, replace kitchen cloths frequently as bacteria build up on these.

Never wash pet bowls along with your own china and always make sure an animal has a separate bowl, tin opener and fork for scooping meat out. Keep pets out of the kitchen if possible. Wash hands after handling them before handling food.

Correct reheating

Many instances of food poisoning result from food being reheated incorrectly. The following guidelines should help avoid the problem.

■ Make sure reheated food is piping hot all the way through. When reheating soups or casseroles on the cooker, make sure they are kept at boiling point for at least five minutes. Foods reheated in a microwave should reach 70°C and be maintained there for two minutes, so always reheat on Full Power (100 per cent). There is further information on the use of a microwave later in this chapter.

■ When leftover food has been reheated and served, any remainder should then be thrown away: only reheat home-cooked or cook/chill foods once.

■ Follow the timing and serving instructions on bought convenience foods carefully, especially cook/chill products.

Safe refrigeration

Invest in a refrigerator thermometer, available from large supermarkets or hardware shops. Check every week or so that this is at the correct temperature: the thermometer should read between 0–5°C in the centre to lower part of the fridge. If it does not, adjust the temperature control accordingly. If the temperature is higher, bacteria will be able to multiply too fast for safe storage.

The bottom of the fridge is the coldest (cold air falls) and the top the warmest. So store uncooked foods, which are most in need of low temperatures, on shelves below cooked foods.

Follow these general rules.

■ Always cover all food, whether raw or cooked, which is put in the fridge. This also preserves the taste because it prevents food from drying out and strong flavours from transferring.

■ Keep cooked and uncooked foods on separate shelves to prevent cross-contamination.

■ Make sure that meat or fish juices – which are very high in bacteria – cannot drip onto other foods, particularly those which will be eaten uncooked. In particular, ensure that salad vegetables cannot be contaminated in this way.

■ Cool leftover foods as quickly as possible, loosely covered with a clean tea cloth so that the steam can escape.

■ Never put warm dishes into the fridge.

■ Do not overcrowd the fridge; let the cold air circulate.

■ Keep the times that the fridge door is opened to a minimum to maintain a safe temperature and save energy.

Safe freezer storage

Similar general rules apply to the maintenance and use of a freezer.

■ Install a thermometer and check regularly that the freezer is at the correct temperature. It should read between –18°C and –22°C.

■ Make sure the door or lid is tightly closed after opening and leave open for the minimum time possible.

■ Label the freezer plug or tape over it so that it is not mistakenly turned off.

■ Pack foods carefully and cover tightly to prevent drying out and freezer burn. Label all packages clearly with the type of food, the date it was put into the freezer and when to use it by.

■ Keep the freezer as full as possible for cost effectiveness (empty space – air – warms quickly so is expensive to keep cold). In the case of a power cut, a full freezer will also stay cold longer and hence the food will be safe for longer.

■ If there is a power cut, do not open the freezer door. Once the power is back on again check over the contents. If they are still hard frozen after a short power cut there is no need for action. Check thoroughly and use up defrosted cooked foods quickly. Raw foods should only be refrozen if first thoroughly cooked through and then cooled.

■ Ensure that foods stored in the freezer are used up regularly. Some items remain good for a shorter time than is generally realised, for instance as a guide freeze these items for these times:

    bacon up to 6 weeks
    salted butter up to 3 months
    meat and poultry up to 6 months
    vegetables and fruit 6–9 months.

After these times foods will still be safe to eat without fear of illness providing they have been frozen and stored correctly, but the quality will deteriorate.

Safe defrosting

It is crucial that frozen food is properly defrosted before use. The guidelines which follow should be noted.

■ Defrost the freezer regularly, every 5–6 months or when ice is beginning to build up. The fridge should also be defrosted regularly unless it is a frost-free model; consult the manufacturer's handbook for directions on how often defrosting is advised.

■ Thaw frozen foods thoroughly in a cold airy place or in the fridge when appropriate. (Never defrost the Christmas turkey in a warm kitchen, since as already stated, bacteria multiply faster in warmth.)

■ Defrost items on a dish or metal tray – anything washable which is large enough to collect drips.

■ Avoid overcrowding as this increases thawing time.

■ Keep foods loosely covered while thawing to shield them from bacteria present in the air.

■ Never try to speed up thawing by putting foods, a frozen chicken for example, into warm water. In an emergency, submerge it in cold water, and change this frequently (although expect the quality to be impaired). Thawing can be carried out in a microwave following manufacturer's directions.

■ Meat and poultry must be completely defrosted before cooking, otherwise it will cook unevenly or may not cook through and any harmful bacteria present will not be destroyed.

Safe microwave cooking

■ Microwaves do not operate evenly throughout the entire oven; consult the manufacturer's handbook as a guide to times required to ensure thorough cooking and reheating with individual makes.

■ Stir foods during cooking as appropriate and do not omit 'standing time' if the recipe recommends it; this is a vital stage in ensuring food cooks or heats through evenly.

■ Microwave ovens vary in output, so check the recipe or packet instructions; recipes are generally tested in a 650 watt model so owners of a 600 watt model should increase the time by 15 seconds for every minute given. Owners of a 700 watt model should reduce the time by 15 seconds for every minute given.

■ Dishes used in the microwave can get hot so check gingerly before lifting them out; a cloth may be needed.

■ Never use dishes with metal rims as these cause sparks and will become blackened.

■ Bottles or containers should never be covered tightly before heating in the microwave. The pressure from the expanding hot air could cause the container to explode.

■ Never attempt to boil an egg in a microwave.

■ Use cling film to cover food in a microwave but ensure that it is pierced so that the steam can escape and make sure it is not in direct contact with food.

■ If cooking more than one item, don't forget to increase the cooking time: for instance, double the cooking time if cooking two jacket potatoes instead of one. Several chicken joints will not cook in the same time as one, as would be the case in a conventional oven, and there would be danger to health in eating them under-cooked.

■ If in any doubt about the performance of your microwave oven, contact the manufacturer without delay.

Safe pressure cooking

■ Check the safety gauges and vents on a pressure cooker from time to time. Replace the rubber seal if it has perished.

■ Always make sure there is sufficient water or liquid before using. As a guide allow ¼pt (150ml) for every 15 minutes of cooking time.

■ Cooking times will vary depending on the size of the food being cooked and the type of foods; for safe use consult the handbook.

■ Never leave the pressure cooker unattended while cooking.

■ Never try to force the lid off; reduce steam quickly by plunging the base of the pressure cooker into a sink of cold water or leave it on a pan stand to reduce pressure slowly then try the lid after 15 minutes. If the handles don't separate easily, leave for a few minutes more.

Safe slow cooking

■ Always preheat a slow cooker before use: check the manufacturer's handbook for the requisite time for thorough cooking of individual dishes.

■ Always make sure foods have been at boiling temperature before they are added to a slow cooker.

■ Avoid taking the lid off, as to compensate for the heat lost you must then add 30 minutes to the cooking time.

■ Both the high and the low setting eventually reach the same temperature: 92°C. The difference between the two settings is the time it takes to reach this temperature.

■ After cooking, remove and chill left-over food quickly. Never leave it in the turned off slow cooker as this provides the warm conditions in which bacteria multiply fast.

4 How labels help

What you can learn

A great deal of information, designed to help shoppers and protect safety, is available on labels.

By law most pre-packed foods must give:

- the name of the food
- a list of ingredients in descending order of weight
- the additives used
- the net weight or volume
- instructions on the storage (if the food is perishable) so that it remains in good condition
- suggestions as to how to make the best use of it, eg cooking times
- the name and address of the manufacturer or supplier
- the place of origin, if failure to give this would mislead the consumer.

For anyone not already used to scanning foods for the information they carry, it would be a useful exercise to look at several labels on products already to hand.

Decreasing order

Once it is known, for instance, that ingredients are listed in decreasing order, there can be some surprises. A favourite strawberry dessert, for instance, may be suddenly revealed to contain more sugar than fruit; far from contributing to the quantity of fruit advisable to eat daily, it can merely prove to be one of the sugary foods which are best avoided.

On this point, it is wise to be alert to the way manufacturers may mislead with their wording. For example, if the label states 'strawberry flavour*ed*' the product must get its flavour from strawberries. If, however, it is described as 'strawberry flavour' the taste does not have to come from strawberries.

Additives

It may also be surprising to find the number of non-foods listed. By popular demand, manufacturers are now greatly reducing the numbers of additives used. But while many were for appearance – such as the very bright colours found in fruit drinks and desserts – many other additives are in convenience foods for a good reason, for instance to extend safe storage time.

The best course for anyone who prefers not to consume so many additives with food or who fears they will not remember the difference between 'strawberry flavour' and 'flavoured' is to switch to fresh ingredients.

Low fat

There is protection for the consumer when manufacturers claim a product is low fat; this must be backed up by nutritional information on the label and show the maximum percentage of that ingredient. It is worth looking at the labels of various types of yogurt, fromage frais and so forth to see how the different manufacturers' products vary.

What's the date?

The aim of providing a date code on products is so that they can be consumed while at their best and with no fear for safety.

All perishable foods – including long-life, canned and frozen products – must now, by law, carry a date mark which tells you when the product is at its best and after which it would be inadvisable to consume it. Always check the date on items (the different forms are explained below). Never buy products past these dates, and at home throw foods away when they have gone past the date.

The *use by, best before* and *best before end* dates cover the period during which a product will be safe to use if it is kept in accordance with the manufacturer's instructions.

Use by

You will find this term used on foods which have a short shelf life and usually need to be kept refrigerated, although there are a few exceptions.

In scientific terms they are microbiologically highly perishable and so are considered likely, after a short period of time, to constitute a danger to human health.

When buying foods with a 'use by' date, it is essential to follow storage instructions, for instance keeping them in the fridge when so directed and using them before the specified date.

Best before and best before end

This term applies to all other foods except certain ones which are exempt (see section on Exempt categories, below).

Products carrying either of these date mark descriptions generally have a longer shelf life than those with a 'use by' date. The length of time can vary from a few weeks to 18 months and over.

It may need a search to find these date codes on canned goods – they may be on the label, printed on the can or embossed on the can end.

Display until

This term is not required by law but it is used by the trade as guidance to shop staff to help good stock rotation. Don't ignore it, however. Look to see if it is accompanied by a 'use by' date. If so, it is crucial that all storage instructions are followed as already explained.

Date codes refer only to the product whilst it is unopened and when it is stored as directed. Some products therefore give additional helpful information on consuming within a certain number of days once opened. A typical instruction might be 'best before 12 September. Once opened, use within two days' or 'use the entire contents of the packet once opened'.

Exempt categories

A few foods do not have to carry a date mark. Some, such as fresh fruit, vegetables and cakes are normally bought for use within a very short period and it is clear when they are deteriorating!

Meat from a butchers' shop, unless it is pre-packed, is also unlikely to carry a date mark. Other products such as alcoholic drinks, sugar, salt and vinegar last for such a long time that a date mark is considered unnecessary. However, if intending to keep long-life foods for several months, it is a wise precaution to write the date of purchase on them before storing in order to follow the procedure of using the earliest bought first.

Knowing your rights

By law, date marks cannot be changed by unauthorised persons and food carrying a 'use by' date must be withdrawn from sale once that date has been passed irrespective of whether the food could be claimed to be wholesome. It is illegal for a store to sell food past its 'use by' date.

On the other hand, it is not an offence to sell food past its 'best before' or 'best before end' date unless it is unfit or has lost its particular properties. However, the Department of Trade discourages the use of any food past its date marking, especially for people at risk, including frail elderly people. If in any doubt about the fitness of food on sale, consult the shop staff.

If after this you are not satisfied, contact:

■ the Trading Standards Department who enforce the laws covering food labelling and food composition, weights and measures, prices and adherence to the Trade Descriptions Act. Contact them via your county, district or borough council which will be listed in The Phone Book.

■ the Environmental Health Department if you are concerned about food hygiene or the contamination of food.

5 | Cost-effective shopping

New plans

Planning the week's shopping needs care: there is a health hazard in buying too much at one time as this could result in left-overs. Food stored beyond its due date brings the chance of food poisoning. Yet for good health it is necessary to buy a wide variety of ingredients to supply all the nutrients needed for healthy bodies. This chapter explores how to go about planning and executing your food shopping with the aim of achieving a healthy balanced diet in the most cost-effective way possible.

The counsel of perfection is to work out meals for the whole week ahead and to organise shopping so dry goods and some perishables are bought at the beginning of the week and further supplies of fresh foods are bought towards the end.

Always start by checking what stores are in the larder cupboards, fridge and freezer already so there is no duplication, then go on to make a list of the things that are needed. A list, which is adhered to, also helps to limit impulse buying.

Where to shop

Where will you find the best value for money? Large supermarkets offer very competitive prices for many basics; flour, oil and so forth are likely to be just as cheap there as at a 'cash and carry' store.

The local butcher may, however, be able to sell meat more cheaply and market stalls are usually considerably cheaper sources of fruit and vegetables. The only general rule is to scan prices constantly, watching out for the special offers posted in different supermarket windows. It is always worthwhile to shop around for the best prices allied to the best quality.

Frozen meat, offal, poultry and fish are cheaper than their fresh counterparts and are also, of course, a good standby. It is cheapest to grow your own herbs – packaged ones, while convenient, are comparatively expensive.

When to shop

There are obvious advantages in choosing to complete the bulk of the shopping in the peaceful off-peak times (late morning or mid-afternoon, mid-week). From the point of view of saving time, this is clearly preferable. To avoid impulse buying, some people find it helpful to use a basket rather than a trolley – putting a physical check on their enthusiasm.

In order to secure the cheapest prices, however, it is worth noting that bargains are commonly available late on Saturday afternoons (in supermarkets which do not open for Sunday trading) since the prices are reduced for meat, dairy products, bread and cakes at that time. Fruit and vegetable stalls in street markets usually start discounting produce from about 4pm depending on locality. If bargains are offered for large quantities, it is wise to underestimate slightly the amount that you know you will be able to use or have energy to cook for freezer stores.

Taking care

When buying frozen foods, make this the last stop of the shopping trip so that the foods will not thaw before being reaching home, which can lead to expensive waste. It is worthwhile investing in a special freezer bag and freezer block to carry with you when shopping to keep foods really cold for a couple of hours. Return the block to the freezer between trips.

Always check the change and receipts you receive when shopping. This is second nature to some, of course, but to anyone unaccustomed to bothering it is wise to remember that market traders tot up prices so quickly that often it's hard to keep up. Check, too, that all bags are stowed away before you leave the stall or store.

It is advisable to look through your receipts on returning home, too; the new itemised type makes it very much easier to spot when just a moment's lack of concentration by a cashier has meant, for instance, that £1.99 has been rung up instead of £1.19.

It could prove helpful, if you want to keep a track of shopping expenses, to keep a separate purse containing the budgeted sum. After a few weeks, review this. It may be that by clever shopping you can manage on a smaller total sum than you originally anticipated.

6 | Your kitchen

EQUIPMENT

New buys and adaptations

Before moving on to a new set of recipes, it is necessary to check what equipment you need to buy and what you can adapt. You may want to get some new items when you see how useful they can be for several recipes.

A steamer for instance makes for very cost-effective cooking. When cooking several vegetables you can avoid the expense of using several rings by cooking, for example, potatoes in a saucepan as usual and another vegetable in a steamer fitted on top. Ideally, you should invest in a saucepan/steamer set, but otherwise you could improvise with a metal colander set over the pan and covered with a tight-fitting lid. Steaming vegetables rather than boiling them is a healthy method of cooking as it means that nutrients are not lost into the cooking water.

An important point to consider when deciding on new kitchen equipment is that retirement may coincide with a time when children have moved away from home and some of your current cookware may be over large. Review it now and consider the possibilities for adaptation. Instead of using a full-size fitted grill pan, for instance, consider grilling a small quantity of food in a small baking tin – or line just half the big grill pan with foil to save on washing up.

There is further information in the recipes which follow on how to cut down on the amount of equipment used – for instance by rinsing out a pan for re-use rather than taking a fresh one. The following equipment is needed for the recipes in this book.

Checklist

Basics

■ Glass mixing bowl and a couple of small basins.

■ Measuring jug.

■ Set of cook's measuring spoons.

■ Rolling pin.

■ Plastic chopping boards (preferably at least two, one for raw and one for cooked meats and ideally a third for fish).

■ Knives, potato peeler, wooden spoon and spatula.

■ Tin opener.

China

■ 1pt (600ml) pie dish.

■ 1¼pt (750ml) soufflé or deep round ovenproof dish.

■ 1¼pt (750ml) gratin-style shallow ovenproof dish.

■ ¾pt (450ml) shallow ovenproof dish.

■ Two large ramekins.

■ Two shallow individual gratin-style dishes.

Pots and pans

■ Medium-sized flameproof and ovenproof casserole with lid for cooker-top and oven cooking.

■ Small saucepan.

■ Larger saucepan.

■ 8in (20cm) nonstick frying pan.

- Colander for draining foods and steaming.
- Small sieve.

Bakeware

- Baking sheet.
- Two small roasting tins, one with a roasting rack for joints, one for roast potatoes.
- 7in (18.5cm) shallow square tin.
- 7in (18.5cm) deep round cake tin.
- 7in (18.5cm) flan tin.
- 1lb (450g) loaf tin.
- 2lb (900g) loaf tin.

Electrical

Preparing fresh foods at home is a healthy alternative to buying some processed foods with their additives and high sugar and salt content.

Many recipes are much easier to prepare with the help of a liquidiser or food processor and with an electric mixer. These save time and effort, especially on puréeing soups, making pastry and breadcrumbs and cake making. Good second-hand offers of these may be found in local papers or, of course, prices may be reduced at sale time.

A microwave oven and a slow cooker have already been mentioned as major kitchen appliances; if you don't have them already it's worth considering investing in them on retirement as in their different ways they can both make for more savings. The speed of microwave cooking, once it is mastered, saves the fuel costs of longer conventional cooking. A slow cooker is economical because the expenditure of electricity is minimal and casseroles can be cooked safely without having the whole oven in operation.

STOCKING UP

A well-stocked store cupboard helps cost-effective cookery. It means the cook can 'stretch' small amounts of expensive ingredients and can also add flavour to dull-tasting but cheap healthy ingredients like lentils to make good meals. The stores in the set of lists can all be kept in the kitchen cupboards or larder, except suet and mayonnaise which need to be kept chilled; there is also a list of ideas for useful items to keep in the freezer.

If, at first glance, the list of stores seems extensive and therefore expensive, don't attempt to re-stock the store cupboard all at once. Adding a few items to the shopping list each week will spread the cost.

Larder stores

Herbs and spices

Mint	Bay leaves	Grated nutmeg
Rosemary	Turmeric	Ground cinnamon and cinnamon sticks
Tarragon	Paprika	
Marjoram	Chilli powder	Cloves
Thyme	Ground cumin	Ground ginger
Sage	Ground coriander	Glacé ginger

Condiments and flavourings

Sunflower oil	Lemon juice	**Stock cubes:**
Wine vinegar	Vanilla essence	chicken
Tomato ketchup and purée	Grated Parmesan cheese	lamb vegetable
Coarse grain mustard	Curry paste or powder	beef
Worcestershire sauce	Soy sauce	

Seeds and nuts

Fennel seeds   Sesame seeds   Almonds

Caraway seeds   Desiccated coconut

Dry goods

Sugar:
caster
granulated
Demerara
icing
soft light brown

Oats:
porridge oats
medium oatmeal

Flour:
plain
self-raising
wholemeal
cornflour

Lentils:
continental green
red

Rice:
long grain white
easy-cook brown
pudding rice

Sultanas
Dried pasta
Raisins
Mixed dried fruit

Cans

Beans:
baked
cannellini
red kidney

Tomatoes
Tuna
Sardines

Apricots
Pineapple

Jars

Honey   Golden syrup

Marmalade   Treacle

Extras

If space allows, it is useful to have dried or long-life milk, and sherry is used to flavour several recipes, though you can use fruit juice instead.

Freezer stores

In a short time a freezer has come close to being regarded as an essential piece of kitchen equipment. However, it does cost money to run. For those on a particularly tight budget, it is sensible to make use of a greater number of store cupboard items above. To make long-term catering more cost-effective, try always to cook extra quantities when making any suitable main dish and freeze the remainder. In addition, buy and store the following:

- frozen meat, fish and vegetables on special offer
- mince or peas in cheap giant size packs and repackaged into smaller bags at home
- bread and other daily basics
- prepared ingredients – a bag of home-made breadcrumbs, a tub of ready chopped parsley or chives, chicken carcass stock, fresh fruit and vegetables when cheap and plentiful, eg blackberries, windfall apples.

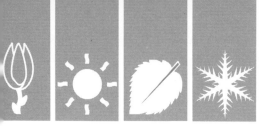

7 | How to use the recipes

Cost

Each of the recipes on the following pages has been costed within defined price categories (see p 53). Clearly, prices may vary according to the season in which a particular recipe is used and where the ingredients are bought.

On the basis of 1992 prices, the total cost of each weekly menu for two people has been estimated at approximately £25.00.

Your choice

The recipes are divided into four sections to correspond with the change in seasons. You will find there are warming dishes for cold winter days, lighter though still filling, healthy meals for spring, and so on.

Each section provides a week's menu with a recipe for a light lunch and more substantial supper and pudding each day. The recipes in the week-long menus are linked, with ingredients remaining from one day being finished off on the next. Opting for the main meal at midday or in the evening is a matter of personal taste and so the recipes can be used accordingly, with, if preferred, the bigger meal at lunchtime and the lighter recipe for supper. Naturally, you can pick and choose between the recipes. If you fancy trying the lunch given for Tuesday, it does not necessarily mean you are committed to eating it on a Tuesday or to following the rest of the menu for the week!

These are merely suggested menus, the choice is yours. However, the menus – and the shopping lists which appear at the end of each section – are costed for a week as a whole. Consequently, choosing recipes selectively may not prove so cost-efficient.

Adapting the recipes

Equally, there is no need to follow the detailed recipes slavishly. Dried pasta is specified, simply because it is the most cost-effective way of buying pasta. If you are free to spend a little more, substitute fresh pasta, now widely on sale. Adjust the cooking times, as it cooks within a minute or two after the water to which it is added returns to the boil. Frozen or dried herbs are specified in the recipes only because fresh herbs bought by the packet are, as already stated, very costly. It is far tastier and much cheaper to grow and use fresh herbs. Again, the recipes stipulate frozen meats and fish throughout, but of course the dishes can be made with freshly bought meat if you choose.

If you are new to cooking you will want to follow the recipes scrupulously. More experienced cooks should feel free to swap ingredients when special offers are available. 'Optional' has been noted by any of the more unusual or more costly ingredients and indicates that you can choose to omit them.

Cooking for one

All the recipes serve two, except those for cakes which keep for several days stored in an airtight tin or which can be frozen. However, the recipes can still be used if you normally cook for one: simply halve the recipes or make up the quantity for two and freeze half for another day.

Mix and match

Included with the recipes is information on when to use ingredients remaining from one meal to prepare part of another. For instance, when egg whites alone are needed in one dish there will be a use for the yolks in another recipe during the week; or if only half a marrow is used, the other half will be presented in a different recipe later.

Extend this principle to mixing and matching your own favourite dishes with these well-balanced, cost-effective recipes.

8 | The recipes

KEY TO THE RECIPE SYMBOLS

COST £
budget beater
(under £1)

Recipes that are quick
to prepare and cook

Shopping tip

Nutritional
information, includ-
ing suitability for a
vegetarian

COST ££
average-priced
recipe (£1–£2)

Cooking method

Ingredients tip

Suggestions for
varying ingredients,
equipment and
cooking methods

COST £££
special meal
(£2–£3)

Freezer information

Uses store ingredients

Tips which give the
expert's way

Sp

SHOPPING LIST

FRUIT AND VEGETABLES

6oz (150g)
button mushrooms

2 leeks

6 carrots

1¼lb (550g)
small onions

6oz (150g)
new potatoes

3¼lb (1.5kg) potatoes

4 medium-sized
baking potatoes

8oz (225g) broccoli

5 tomatoes

8oz (225g)
white cabbage

1 small iceberg lettuce

1 cauliflower

1 bunch watercress

1 lemon

1 orange

1 grapefruit

1¾lb (775g)
cooking apples

12oz (325g) rhubarb

1 small banana

2 kiwi fruit

DAIRY PRODUCE

2pt (1.2 litre)
semi-skimmed milk

6oz (150g)
set natural yogurt

8oz (225g)
Cheddar cheese

11 eggs

1lb (450g) margarine

¼pt (150ml)
whipping cream

MEAT AND FISH

12oz (325g)
streaky bacon

1lb (450g) pork ribs

8oz (225g) minced beef

2 medium herrings

FROZEN FOODS

4 lambs' kidneys

8oz (225g) tub
chicken livers

3lb 12oz (1.7kg)
chicken with giblets

7oz (200g) sweetcorn

6oz (150g) leaf spinach

1lb (450g) puff pastry

2tsp chopped chives

BREAD

1 Granary loaf

ring

CANS AND DRY GOODS

8oz (225g) can
baked beans

7oz (198g) can
tuna chunks in brine

4oz (100g) red lentils

14oz (397g) can tomatoes

11oz (425g) can
low-fat custard

4oz (100g) long grain rice

4oz (100g) penne or
other dried pasta shapes

14½oz (411g) can apricot
halves

2tbsp grated Parmesan

6oz (150g) plain flour

6oz (150g)
self-raising flour

10oz (275g) caster sugar

½oz (15g)
granulated sugar

8oz (225g)
demerara sugar

6oz (150g)
soft light brown sugar

4oz (100g)
porridge oats

STORE CUPBOARD

7fl oz (210ml)
sunflower oil

1tbsp tomato purée

3tbsp tomato ketchup

10 garlic cloves

1tbsp
Worcestershire sauce

1tsp cornflour

2tbsp icing sugar

4tbsp golden syrup

1tbsp lemon juice

4tbsp reduced-calorie
mayonnaise

3tbsp medium oatmeal

2tbsp desiccated coconut

½ tsp vanilla essence

4tsp hot
curry paste or powder

2 vegetable stock cubes

2½ tsp white wine or
distilled malt vinegar

3oz (75g) sultanas

2tbsp sherry, optional

HERBS AND SPICES

½ tsp ground cumin

¾ tsp ground coriander

1¼ tsp ground ginger

pinch grated nutmeg

1tsp ground cinnamon

1tsp paprika

¼ tsp chilli powder

½ tsp caraway seeds

1½ tsp turmeric

2 bay leaves

¼ tsp dried tarragon

Roast chicken

COST £££

High protein.

Frozen chickens are cheaper than fresh.

Make sure chicken is thoroughly defrosted before cooking and always remove bag of giblets!

1¼lb (550g) potatoes
3tbsp sunflower oil
3lb 12oz (1.7kg)
frozen chicken, defrosted
½ orange
¼tsp dried tarragon
1oz (25g) margarine

1 onion
2oz (50g) button mushrooms
2oz (50g) breadcrumbs
1 egg yolk
2tbsp plain flour

1 Preheat oven to 400°F, 200°C, Gas 6. Peel and cut potatoes into two or three pieces and cook in boiling, lightly salted water for 4–5 minutes until just tender.

2 Put 2tbsp oil into a roasting tin. Drain potatoes well, reserving 1pt (600ml) of cooking water, and add potatoes to roasting tin. Toss in oil and cook on shelf above centre of oven.

3 Remove giblets from chicken. Rinse chicken inside and out with cold water and drain well. Put into a second roasting tin.

4 Grate orange rind and reserve for stuffing. Squeeze juice over chicken and put squeezed orange half inside chicken. Re-truss. Sprinkle chicken with seasoning and tarragon and dot with margarine.

5 Roast chicken on shelf below potatoes for 50 minutes.

6 Put giblets into a saucepan with reserved potato water. Chop half an onion and add to pan with seasoning. Bring to boil and simmer for 40 minutes. Strain and reserve.

7 Meanwhile, make stuffing. Finely chop other half of onion and mushrooms. Fry in remaining 1tbsp oil for 5 minutes, stirring occasionally.

8 Remove from heat and stir in breadcrumbs, reserved orange rind, egg yolk and seasoning. Cool slightly then shape into six small balls.

9 Turn potatoes and spoon oil over. Add stuffing balls to chicken roasting tin and spoon juices over. Cook for 20 minutes.

10 Swap oven positions so chicken is on top shelf and cook for 20 minutes more until browned.

11 Drain chicken and stuffing balls and transfer to a serving plate. Drain potatoes and arrange around chicken. Keep hot.

12 Pour off all but 2tbsp juices from chicken roasting tin and stir in flour. Cook for 1 minute then stir in giblet stock and bring to the boil, stirring. Strain into a gravy boat and serve with chicken and Steamed vegetable medley.

■ **Save left-over chicken for lunch the following day and use the carcass to make stock.**

SUNDAY LUNCH

Steamed vegetable medley

COST £

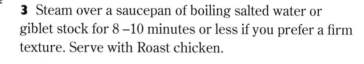

Look out for bargain
buys at the end of the
Saturday market.

Cook vegetables just
before serving so
they don't go soggy.

¹/₂ cauliflower

4oz (100g) broccoli   1 carrot

1 Cut cauliflower and broccoli into florets, slice broccoli stalks thickly.

2 Peel and cut carrot into matchstick strips.

3 Steam over a saucepan of boiling salted water or giblet stock for 8 –10 minutes or less if you prefer a firm texture. Serve with Roast chicken.

SUNDAY PUDDING

Kiwi pavlova

COST ££

Try Greek yogurt
instead of cream; it
looks the same but
there's a little less fat.

3 egg whites or equivalent dried egg white

6oz (150g) caster sugar

¹/₂ tsp vanilla essence

¹/₂ tsp white wine vinegar (or distilled malt)

1 tsp cornflour

TOPPING

¹/₄ pt (150ml) whipping cream

2 kiwi fruit

1 Preheat the oven to 225° F, 110° C, Gas ¹/₄. Line a baking sheet with a large piece of non-stick baking paper and, using a plate as a guide, draw a 7in (18.5cm) circle.

2 Whisk egg whites in a large bowl until stiff, moist-looking peaks form, or reconstitute and use dried egg whites according to manufacturer's instructions. Gradually whisk in sugar 1tsp at a time and continue whisking for several minutes until meringue mixture is very thick and glossy.

In summer, use raspberries or a mixture of berries.

3 Mix vanilla essence, vinegar and cornflour together in a cup and then whisk into meringue mixture.

4 Spoon on to paper-lined baking sheet and spread to a rough circle. Cook for 1 hour or until paper may be peeled away from base of pavlova. Leave to cool on paper in turned off oven, leaving door slightly ajar.

When pavlova is cooked, paper will peel away from base easily. If not, cook longer.

5 Remove paper from pavlova and transfer to a serving plate. Two hours before serving, whip cream until softly peaking and spoon over pavlova.

6 Peel kiwi fruits and slice crossways. Arrange on top of pavlova. Cut into large wedges to serve. Best eaten 2 hours after completing with cream.

■ **To test if egg whites are sufficiently whisked, turn bowl upside down. If you think they'll fall out . . . they need more whisking.**

Flapjacks

COST £

Quick to make.

Freeze up to 3 months in a plastic bag.

Store cupboard ingredients.

4oz (100g) margarine

4oz (100g) soft light brown sugar

4tbsp golden syrup

4oz (100g) porridge oats

2oz (50g) self-raising flour

1 Preheat oven to 350° F, 180° C, Gas 4. Lightly oil a 7in (18.5cm) shallow square tin.

2 Put margarine, sugar and syrup in a saucepan and heat until margarine has melted.

3 Remove from heat and stir in oats and flour. Spoon into tin and level surface.

4 Cook for 25 minutes until browned. Remove from oven and leave to cool for 15 minutes. Mark into bars and leave to cool completely.

Use level measuring spoons of syrup. Mixture will appear soft when it first comes out of oven, but hardens on cooling.

Bacon and kidney kebabs

4 frozen lambs' kidneys, defrosted
4 rashers streaky bacon
1 tbsp tomato ketchup
1 tbsp sunflower oil
1 tbsp Worcestershire sauce
8oz (225g) can baked beans

COST ££

High in iron.

Stretch bacon to make it go further.

Could use cocktail sausages in place of or along with kidneys.

1 Rinse kidneys with cold water and drain well. Cut each into quarters and cut away white core.

2 Derind and stretch each rasher of bacon by pressing the back of a knife on one end of bacon and then running it along, until rasher length is almost doubled.

3 Cut each rasher in 4 and wrap each piece around a kidney quarter. Thread on to 2 long metal skewers.

4 Put kebabs on a piece of foil on grill rack. Mix ketchup, oil and Worcestershire sauce together in a cup and brush over kebabs.

5 Cook under a hot grill for 15 minutes, turning once and brushing with remaining ketchup mixture until bacon is crisp.

6 Meanwhile, heat baked beans in a small saucepan. Spoon on to serving plates and add kebabs.

Chicken and sweetcorn pie

COST £

Could use homemade
shortcrust pastry.

½ orange, juice only
remaining gravy from
Sunday
¼ – ½ pt (150–300ml)
semi-skimmed milk
1 leek
chicken left-overs
from Sunday
1oz (25g) margarine

1oz (25g) plain flour
¼ tsp ground coriander
2oz (50g) frozen sweetcorn
8oz (225g) frozen
puff pastry, defrosted
1 whole egg or
egg yolk to glaze
4 carrots

1 Put orange juice and any gravy into a measuring jug and make up to ½pt (300ml) with milk.

2 Trim and slit leek, wash and then slice thinly. Take meat off chicken carcass and dice, discarding skin. (Save carcass for soup, see Tuesday lunch.)

3 Heat margarine in a saucepan, add leek and fry for 3 minutes, stirring until softened.

4 Stir in flour and coriander and cook for 1 minute. Add milk mixture and bring to the boil, stirring continuously until sauce is thickened and smooth.

5 Stir chicken and sweetcorn into sauce. Season well and cook for 2 minutes. Spoon into a 1¼pt (750ml) pie dish. Leave to cool slightly.

6 Preheat oven to 425°F, 220°C, Gas 7. Roll out pastry on a lightly floured surface until a little larger than top of pie dish.

7 Brush edge of pie dish with water. Cut a strip of pastry and press on to rim. Brush pastry strip with water.

8 Lift remaining pastry over the rolling pin and position on dish. Seal edges together, trim, knock up and crimp (for method, see tip below). Reroll trimmings and make leaves to decorate pie, or mark whole top lightly with a knife to give a criss cross pattern. Make two small cuts in centre.

9 Brush pie with beaten egg and cook for 35 minutes, covering with foil if overbrowning after 25 minutes.

10 Meanwhile, slice carrots and cook in boiling, lightly salted water for 15 minutes. Drain and serve with the pie.

■ **To knock up and crimp, make small horizontal cuts along pastry side edge where lid and pastry strip meet. To crimp, press finger and thumb of left hand along top surface of pastry edge and make small vertical cuts between fingertips.**

PUDDING MONDAY

Caramelised grapefruit

1 grapefruit
2tbsp demerara or light brown sugar

generous pinch ground ginger

1 Halve grapefruit and loosen segments with a small knife. Put halves into a shallow ovenproof dish.

2 Sprinkle with sugar and ginger and cook at 425°F, 220°C, Gas 7 on shelf below Chicken and sweetcorn pie for 20 minutes until sugar has caramelised. Serve hot.

COST £

If watching calories, choose sweeter ruby grapefruit and omit the sugar or use half the quantity.

Quick to prepare.

High in vitamin C.

Can grill instead.

French onion soup

COST £

When you don't have a carcass for stock, use a stock cube.

Store cupboard ingredients.

1 chicken carcass
12oz (325g) small onions
1tbsp sunflower oil
1tsp granulated sugar
1 garlic clove, crushed

TOPPING
2 slices Granary toast
1 garlic clove, halved
2oz (50g) Cheddar cheese

1 Put chicken carcass in a deep saucepan with 2pt (1.2 litre) water and seasoning. Bring to the boil, cover and simmer for 1 hour.

2 Strain stock into a bowl and reserve. Discard carcass. Halve and thinly slice onions.

3 Wash and dry pan and heat oil. Add onions and fry gently for 10 minutes, stirring occasionally, until softened.

4 Add sugar and garlic and increase the heat. Fry, stirring frequently, for 10–15 minutes until onions are deep brown.

5 Add strained stock and seasoning and simmer for 30 minutes.

6 Cut each slice of toast in four and rub each piece with a cut garlic clove. Grate cheese.

7 Spoon soup into bowls, float bread on top and sprinkle with cheese, grill until cheese has melted and serve at once.

Grilled herrings in oatmeal

2 medium-sized herring, heads removed, gutted

6oz (150g) new potatoes

2tbsp semi-skimmed milk

3tbsp medium oatmeal

2 tomatoes

4oz (100g) broccoli

COST ££

Ask fishmonger to bone fish for you.

1 Enlarge slit along belly of each herring towards tail. Cut around bones and backbone and remove. Rinse inside of fish well with cold water and drain. Place fish, skin side uppermost and open out, press flat with the heel of the hand.

2 Scrub and halve any large potatoes. Cook in a saucepan of boiling, lightly salted water for 15 minutes until tender.

Include oily fish in the diet at least once a week.

3 Put milk on one plate and oatmeal on a second plate. Dip herring, flesh side downwards into milk then oatmeal. Season well and sprinkle any remaining oatmeal over.

Could use mackerel in place of herrings.

4 Put skin-side downwards in base of grill pan with halved tomatoes. Cook under a hot grill for 8–10 minutes until oatmeal is browned and fish flakes when pressed with a knife.

5 Meanwhile, cut broccoli into florets and cook in potato pan for last 5 minutes of cooking.

6 Transfer herrings and tomatoes to serving plates. Drain potatoes and broccoli and spoon on to plates.

TUESDAY PUDDING

Hot apple salad

Can make with
dessert apples and
bananas, too.

12oz (325g) cooking apples
½tsp ground coriander
½oz (15g) margarine

2tbsp demerara sugar
or honey
2tbsp desiccated coconut

1 Quarter, core and peel apples. Slice thinly and put into a shallow ovenproof dish or sandwich tin. Sprinkle coriander over, add sugar or honey and dot with margarine.

2 Cook under a hot grill for 7–8 minutes, turning once until apples are tender.

3 Sprinkle with coconut and cook for 2–3 minutes until lightly toasted. Stir and spoon into serving bowls. Serve hot with ice cream if liked.

WEDNESDAY LUNCH

Tuna pâté

COST £

Look out for cheaper
canned tuna chunks.

7oz (198g) can tuna chunks
in brine
2tbsp reduced-calorie
mayonnaise
1tbsp lemon juice

2 tsp fresh or frozen
chopped chives
¼ iceberg lettuce
crusty Granary bread

1 Drain tuna and spoon into a bowl. Add mayonnaise, 1tsp lemon juice and seasoning and beat together until almost smooth. Stir in chives (optional).

2 Finely shred lettuce, toss in remaining lemon juice and seasoning and spoon on to serving plates. Top with tuna. Serve with warm Granary bread.

Part-cooked rolls make a handy freezer standby. No need to thaw before baking.

Tuna is a cheap source of protein. Buy tuna in brine to save calories.

SUPPER WEDNESDAY

Sticky ribs

1lb (450g) pork ribs
1tbsp sunflower oil
2tbsp tomato ketchup
1tsp paprika
$^1/_2$tsp ground cumin
$^1/_4$tsp chilli powder
2 medium-sized baking potatoes

COLESLAW
8oz (225g) white cabbage
1 carrot
2tbsp reduced-calorie mayonnaise
2tbsp set natural yogurt
$^1/_2$tsp caraway seeds, optional
$^1/_2$oz (15g) margarine

COST £££

Weight-watchers can omit mayonnaise from coleslaw, add more yogurt and serve potatoes without added fat.

1 Preheat oven to 400°F, 200°C, Gas 6. Line a small roasting tin with foil and add ribs.

2 Mix oil, ketchup, paprika, cumin, chilli and seasoning together and spoon over ribs.

3 Cook ribs on shelf just above centre of oven for 1$^1/_4$ hours. Turn ribs halfway through cooking and brush with pan juice mixture.

4 Prick potatoes and cook alongside ribs for 1$^1/_4$ hours.

Lining grill pan with foil saves washing up!

5 Meanwhile, make coleslaw. Finely shred cabbage, discarding woody central core. Grate carrot and put cabbage, carrot, mayonnaise, yogurt, caraway seeds, if using, and seasoning into a bowl and mix together.

6 Cut open potatoes and add a knob of margarine to each. Arrange on serving plates with ribs and coleslaw.

WEDNESDAY PUDDING

Lemon puddle pudding

COST **£**

Store cupboard
ingredients.

Fold egg whites in
carefully so you don't
knock out all the air.

2 eggs

1½oz (40g) self-raising flour

2oz (50g) caster sugar

2oz (50g) soft margarine

1 lemon

6 fl oz (180ml)
semi-skimmed milk

1 Lightly grease a 1¼pt (750ml) soufflé or deep ovenproof dish.

2 Separate eggs, put yolks, flour, sugar and margarine into a bowl. Grate rind and squeeze juice from lemon. Add rind to bowl and whisk ingredients together.

3 Gradually whisk in milk then lemon juice.

4 Whisk egg whites in a separate bowl until softly peaking then fold into lemon mixture.

5 Pour into soufflé dish and put dish in a roasting tin. Pour boiling water into tin to come half way up sides of soufflé dish. Cook at 400°F, 200°C, Gas 6 on shelf below ribs for 45–50 minutes until well risen like a soufflé and golden brown. There will be a sauce layer at the bottom.

6 Spoon into bowls and serve hot.

■ **Mixture may look curdled, this will disappear with cooking.**

Eggs florentine

6oz (150g) frozen
leaf spinach, defrosted

¹/₂oz (15g) margarine

¹/₂oz (15g) plain flour

¹/₄pt (150ml)
semi-skimmed milk

pinch grated nutmeg

2oz (50g) Cheddar cheese

2 eggs

1tbsp fresh breadcrumbs

buttered toast

COST £

Always buy eggs from a supermarket with a fast turnover.

High protein.

To use fresh spinach: wash, discard stalks, stir fry 1–2 min until just wilted. Continue as above.

1 Put spinach into a sieve and squeeze out liquid with the back of a spoon. Put spinach into a bowl.

2 Melt margarine in a saucepan. Stir in flour and cook for 1 minute. Add milk and bring to the boil, stirring until thickened and smooth.

3 Stir nutmeg and seasoning into sauce. Add 3tbsp of sauce to spinach, mix together then divide between 2 small shallow ovenproof dishes and spread over base of dishes.

4 Grate cheese and stir half into remaining sauce. Set aside.

5 Half fill a deep frying pan with water and bring to the boil. Break each egg into a cup then slide into the water. Cook gently (bubbles should be just breaking the surface of the water) until whites are opaque and yolks are set.

6 Carefully lift eggs out of pan with a draining spoon, trim whites to neaten and put on top of spinach. Spoon sauce over and sprinkle with remaining cheese and breadcrumbs.

7 Cook under a hot grill for 8–10 minutes until heated through and topping is golden. Serve hot with buttered toast.

Mixed vegetable dhal

COST £

Vary vegetables depending on bargain buys.

Suitable for vegetarians.

Naan breads and pittas are comparatively expensive but make a good alternative to rice.

I small onion
12oz (325g) potatoes
¹/₂ cauliflower
1tbsp sunflower oil
2 garlic cloves, crushed
1tsp turmeric

2tsp hot curry paste or powder
4oz (100g) red lentils
1¹/₄pt (750ml) vegetable stock
4oz (100g) long grain rice

1 Thinly slice onion. Scrub and dice potatoes. Cut any cauliflower leaves into thick slices and cauliflower into florets.

2 Heat oil in a saucepan, add onion and fry for 5 minutes until lightly browned. Add potatoes, cauliflower florets, garlic and turmeric and fry, stirring, for 2–3 minutes.

3 Add curry paste or powder, lentils, stock and seasoning. Bring to the boil, cover and simmer for 20 minutes, stirring occasionally, until lentils and vegetables are just tender.

4 Meanwhile, cook rice in a saucepan of boiling, lightly salted water for 10 minutes until just tender. Drain, rinse with hot water and drain again. Keep hot.

5 Add cauliflower leaves to curry mixture, cover and cook for 2–3 minutes until softened.

6 Spoon dhal into bowls and serve with rice.

Rhubarb and ginger fool

12oz (325g) rhubarb
2oz (50g) caster sugar
¹/₄ tsp ground ginger

¹/₂ x 15oz (425g) can low-fat custard
4tbsp set natural yogurt

COST £ £

Quick to prepare.

1 Trim and discard leaves from rhubarb. Wash stalks and slice. Put into a saucepan with the sugar and ginger. Cover and cook gently, shaking pan from time to time until soft but still brightly coloured. Cool.

2 Transfer rhubarb to a bowl, stir in custard and yogurt and then spoon into glass dishes. Chill until required.

Reserve remaining half can of custard for Apricot upside-down pudding on Friday.

Make custard with milk and custard powder.

If cooked rhubarb looks a little dark, brighten with a few drops of red food colouring.

Penne with mushroom and tomato sauce

COST £ £

Quick to make.

Suitable for vegetarians if vegetarian Cheddar is used.

Reheats well in the microwave in serving dishes.

4oz (100g) penne or other pasta shapes

1 leek or onion

4oz (100g) button mushrooms

1tbsp sunflower oil

2 garlic cloves, crushed

14oz (397g) can tomatoes

¹/₄ tsp sugar

2tbsp Parmesan or grated Cheddar cheese

1 Cook pasta in a saucepan of boiling, lightly salted water for 10–12 minutes until just tender.

2 Meanwhile, trim and slit leek, wash and slice thinly. If using an onion, chop finely. Slice mushrooms.

3 Heat oil in a second saucepan, add leeks or onion and mushrooms and fry for 5 minutes, stirring occasionally.

4 Add garlic, tomatoes, sugar and seasoning and simmer for 10 minutes until thick.

5 Drain pasta and add to sauce. Toss together and divide between 2 dishes. Sprinkle with grated cheese and serve hot.

Bobotie

2 medium-sized
baking potatoes

8oz (225g) lean minced beef

1 small onion

1 small banana

1 garlic clove, crushed

4tbsp fresh breadcrumbs

2tsp curry paste or powder

2tsp vinegar

1tbsp tomato purée

1oz (25g) sultanas

oil for brushing tin

2 bay leaves

1 egg

pinch turmeric

4tbsp semi-skimmed milk

2 tomatoes

3oz (75g) frozen sweetcorn

COST £ £

Buy lean mince and
drain fat off after
cooking to keep fat
to a minimum.

Much easier to shape
foil loosely over base
of tin, then put inside
tin.

1 Preheat oven to 375° F, 190° C, Gas 5. Prick potatoes
and push a skewer through the centre of each. Cook on
shelf above the centre of the oven for 1¼ hours.

2 Meanwhile, dry fry mince in a saucepan. Chop onion
and banana. Add onion to pan and cook, stirring until
mince is evenly browned. Drain off any fat.

3 Remove from heat and stir in banana, garlic,
breadcrumbs, curry paste or powder, vinegar,
tomato purée, sultanas and seasoning.

4 Line a 1lb (450g) loaf tin with foil (or use a china dish
and don't line). Brush with oil. Spoon in mince mixture
and level surface. Arrange bay leaves on top.

5 Cook on shelf below centre of oven for 20 minutes.

6 Beat egg, turmeric and milk together and pour over
mince mixture. Cook for a further 20 minutes.

7 Halve tomatoes and put in a shallow ovenproof dish
and season. Cook on shelf alongside potatoes for 10
minutes. Cook sweetcorn in a saucepan of boiling water
for 5 minutes. Drain.

8 Carefully turn out and peel away foil, or leave in china dish. Cut into thick slices. Arrange on serving plates with jacket potatoes, tomatoes and sweetcorn.

FRIDAY PUDDING

Apricot upside-down pudding

COST ££

Quick to prepare.

Remaining pudding freezes well, wrapped in foil, for up to 3 months.

Store cupboard ingredients.

4tbsp demerara sugar
14¼oz (411g) can apricot halves, drained

TOPPING
4oz (100g) soft margarine
4oz (100g) demerara or caster sugar
4oz (100g) self-raising flour
1tsp ground ginger
2 eggs

1 Grease and base line a 7in (18.5cm) shallow square tin with greased greaseproof paper.

2 Sprinkle 4tbsp demerara sugar over base of tin. Drain apricots well and arrange cut side uppermost on top of sugar.

3 Put all topping ingredients in a bowl and mix together until smooth.

4 Spoon over apricots and level surface. Cook alongside Bobotie at 375°F, 190°C, Gas 5 for 25–30 minutes until sponge is well risen and it springs back when pressed with the fingertips.

5 Loosen edge of sponge with a knife then turn out on to a serving plate. Cut into squares and serve warm with custard remaining from Thursday.

Warm chicken liver salad

8oz (225g) tub frozen
chicken livers, just defrosted

½ iceberg lettuce

½ bunch watercress

1 tomato

1oz (25g) margarine

1tbsp sunflower oil

1 garlic clove, crushed,
optional

2tbsp sherry or stock

1 Put chicken livers in a sieve and wash thoroughly with cold water. Drain and roughly chop, discarding any white parts.

2 Tear lettuce into small pieces. Pick over watercress and discard long stalks. Cut tomato into thin wedges and divide salad vegetables between two plates.

3 Heat margarine and oil in a frying pan. Add garlic, if using, and chicken livers and cook over a high heat, stirring constantly, for 4 minutes until evenly browned.

4 Add sherry or stock and seasoning and cook for 1 minute. Spoon mixture over salad and serve immediately.

COST ££

High in iron.
To reduce fat, use
only oil and fry in a
non-stick pan.

Store remaining
watercress in a blown
up plastic bag in the
fridge.

Cheesy potato bake

COST ££

Can be prepared earlier in the day and reheated thoroughly when required.

If sauce goes lumpy, whisk until smooth.

1¼lb (550g) potatoes
6oz (150g) streaky bacon or bacon pieces
4oz (100g) Cheddar cheese
2oz (50g) margarine
2oz (50g) plain flour
¾pt (450ml) semi-skimmed milk

2 garlic cloves, crushed
2oz (50g) frozen sweetcorn, defrosted
2tbsp fresh breadcrumbs
½ bunch watercress, optional

1 Preheat oven to 425° F, 220° C, Gas 7. Thinly slice potatoes and cook in a saucepan of boiling, lightly salted water for 4–5 minutes until just tender. Drain, rinse with cold water and drain again.

2 Derind and grill bacon until crisp then dice. Grate cheese.

3 Rinse and dry potato pan and melt margarine in it. Stir in flour and cook for 1 minute. Gradually add milk and bring to the boil, stirring continuously until thickened and smooth.

4 Stir in 3oz (75g) of the cheese, garlic and seasoning.

5 Spread half the potatoes over the base of a shallow ovenproof dish, add bacon and sweetcorn. Pour over half the sauce.

6 Overlap remaining potatoes over the top. Spoon sauce over to cover completely. Sprinkle with remaining cheese and breadcrumbs.

7 Cook on shelf just above centre of the oven for 30 minutes until well browned. Spoon on to plates and garnish with sprigs of watercress.

Apple strudel

2oz (50g) soft
light brown or caster sugar

1tsp ground cinnamon

2 medium-sized
cooking apples

2oz (50g) sultanas

8oz (225g) frozen
puff pastry, defrosted

2tbsp semi-skimmed milk

2tbsp icing sugar

COST £

1 Mix sugar and cinnamon in a bowl. Quarter, core and peel apples. Cut into very thin crossways slices and add to bowl with sultanas. Mix together and set aside.

2 Roll out pastry thinly on a lightly floured surface and trim to a 12in (30cm) square.

3 Spoon apple mixture over, leaving a 1in (2.5cm) border of pastry. Brush pastry edge with milk. Roll up, seal edges well and twist ends. Make a couple of cuts in centre top.

4 Put on to a greased baking sheet and brush with remaining milk. Cook at 425°F, 220°C, Gas 7 on shelf above Cheesy potato bake for 30 minutes until golden brown. Sprinkle with sifted icing sugar and cut into thick slices to serve.

Swap Cheesy potato bake and Apple strudel over, if strudel is overbrowning.

Could also use pears, or pears and apples mixed.

Freeze up to 6 months in a polybag.

■ **Traditionally, this is made with strudel or filo pastry, which is tricky to make, but is now available ready-rolled and sold in the freezer section of many supermarkets. To use, overlap four sheets to form one large piece before adding apples.**

Su

SHOPPING LIST

FRUIT AND VEGETABLES

6 small onions

10 carrots

1 large head of celery

8 oz (225g) button mushrooms

1 small marrow about 2lb (900g)

1 bunch or packet watercress

½ cucumber

9 tomatoes

1 lettuce

1lb (450g) baby new potatoes

6oz (150g) green cabbage

8oz (225g) plums

2 kiwi fruit

2 bananas

2 dessert apples

2 nectarines

4 oranges

6oz (150g) strawberries

4oz (100g) blackcurrants

DAIRY PRODUCE

3oz (75g) Cheddar cheese

7oz (200g) red Leicester or extra Cheddar

4oz (100g) low-fat soft cheese

1pt 12fl oz (960ml) semi-skimmed milk

7oz (200g) natural yogurt

12 eggs

10½oz (290g) margarine

MEAT AND FISH

2oz (50g) sliced garlic sausage or ham

4oz (100g) lean minced beef

8oz (225g) boneless pork chump chop

8oz (225g) herby pork sausages

4 chicken drumsticks

6oz (150g) smoked mackerel fillets

2 small trout

FROZEN FOODS

2 scoops vanilla ice cream

2oz (50g) sweetcorn

14oz (400g) peas

12oz (325g) smoked haddock

2tbsp chives or parsley

mmer

BREAD AND BISCUITS

1 small wholemeal loaf

6 thin slices white bread

1 small French bread stick

7oz (200g) Nice biscuits

1oz (25g) macaroon biscuits

CANS AND DRY GOODS

8oz (227g) can tomatoes

10oz (283g) can broad beans

4oz (100g) self-raising flour

2oz (50g) plain flour

8oz (225g) wholemeal flour

1½oz (40g) icing sugar

2oz (50g) caster sugar

7oz (200g) granulated sugar

4oz (100g) long grain white rice

6oz (150g) easy-cook brown rice

2oz (50g) unblanched almonds

6oz (150g) plain chocolate-flavoured cake covering

3oz (75g) sultanas

1tbsp grated Parmesan

STORE CUPBOARD

10tbsp sunflower oil

8tbsp tomato ketchup

2tbsp soy sauce

3 garlic cloves

3tbsp sherry, optional

4tsp wine vinegar

1tsp hot curry paste or powder

½ beef stock cube

½ chicken stock cube

1½tsp coarse grain mustard

2tbsp reduced-calorie mayonnaise

5tsp sesame seeds

¼ tsp vanilla essence

5tsp lemon juice

2tbsp apricot jam or marmalade

3tbsp golden syrup

1tbsp chopped glacé ginger

HERBS AND SPICES

¼ tsp dried marjoram

½ tsp dried sage

4tsp fresh mint or ½ tsp dried mint

1 bay leaf

½ tsp dried thyme

1½ tsp paprika

¾ tsp turmeric

½ tsp fennel seeds

¼ tsp ground cinnamon

pinch grated nutmeg

¼ tsp ground ginger

Grilled trout with fennel

COST £££

Quick to cook.

Shop around for trout
as prices vary.

To test if trout is
cooked, pierce with a
knife through gutted
area, flesh should
break easily and be
opaque.

8oz (225g) baby
new potatoes

2 small trout,
gutted and cleaned

1 tbsp sunflower oil

1 tbsp lemon juice

¹/₄ tsp fennel seeds

4oz (100g) frozen
peas

2 tomatoes

¹/₄ lettuce

1 Scrub potatoes, halve any large ones and cook in a
saucepan of boiling, lightly salted water for 20 minutes.

2 Meanwhile, rinse trout inside and out with cold water
then drain well. Make a foil tray just a little bigger than
the trout and put in base of grill pan.

3 Put trout on foil, brush with oil, sprinkle lemon juice
over and season well.

4 Crush fennel seeds with a pestle and mortar. Sprinkle
on top of and inside trout. Grill for 10 minutes, turning
once until browned and fish flakes when pressed with a
knife.

5 Meanwhile, cook peas for 5 minutes in a small
saucepan of boiling, lightly salted water. Dice tomatoes,
finely shred lettuce.

6 Drain potatoes and spoon on to two serving plates.
Carefully lift each trout on to the serving plates and
spoon a little of the juices over the trout. Keep hot.

7 Drain peas and set aside. Add remaining trout juices to pan. Add tomatoes and cook for 2–3 minutes until soft. Return peas to pan, add lettuce and cook for 30 seconds until lettuce is warm. Toss together, spoon on to plates and serve immediately.

■ **If you don't have a pestle and mortar, use a cup and crush seeds with the end of a rolling pin.**

PUDDING SUNDAY

Crème caramel

3oz (75g) granulated sugar

1 egg

2 egg yolks

2tbsp caster sugar

½pt (300ml) semi-skimmed milk

few drops vanilla essence

COST £

Store cupboard ingredients.

Best made the day before.

1 Preheat oven to 325°F, 160°C, Gas 3. Warm 2 large ramekin dishes in the bottom of the oven. Put granulated sugar and 3tbsp water in a heavy based saucepan and heat gently, without stirring, until sugar has dissolved.

2 Increase heat and boil sugar rapidly for a few minutes until golden brown. Plunge base of pan into cold water to stop cooking and when bubbles subside, swirl pan to mix syrup.

3 Quickly pour caramel into ramekins and tilt dishes until base and sides are evenly coated.

4 Lightly whisk egg, egg yolks and caster sugar together. Pour milk into a small saucepan and bring just to the boil. Whisk milk into egg mixture, add vanilla and then strain mixture into ramekin dishes.

5 Stand ramekin dishes in a small roasting tin and pour hot water into tin to come half way up the sides of the dishes.

6 Cook, uncovered, in centre of oven for 35 minutes until well set. To test, insert a knife into the centre, if it comes out cleanly then it's cooked. Double check by tapping sides of dishes, custard should wobble like a jelly if set.

7 Remove from roasting tin and leave to cool, transfer to the fridge until ready to serve.

8 To turn out, loosen edge of custard with fingertip then run a knife around edges and turn out on to shallow serving dishes.

■ If you don't have ramekins, use thick china cups instead.
■ If puddings won't turn out, dip base of ramekin in boiling water for a few seconds to melt caramel.

SUNDAY TEA

No-bake chocolate cake

COST ££

Quick to make.

6oz (150g) plain chocolate-flavoured cake covering
2oz (50g) margarine
3tbsp golden syrup

7oz (200g) Nice biscuits
1tbsp chopped glacé ginger
3oz (75g) sultanas

1 Line base and sides of a 7in (18.5cm) shallow square tin with greaseproof paper.

2 Break chocolate into pieces and put into a saucepan with margarine and syrup. Heat gently, stirring occasionally, until melted.

3 Remove chocolate mixture from the heat. Put biscuits into a plastic bag and crush into small pieces with a rolling pin.

4 Stir biscuits, ginger and sultanas into chocolate mixture and continue stirring until evenly coated in chocolate.

5 Spoon into tin and level surface. Chill for 2–3 hours until set.

6 Lift paper out of tin and peel away. Cut mixture into small squares to serve.

Freeze remaining squares in a plastic box, interleaved with greaseproof paper, for up to 3 months.

Pizza fingers

COST £

If you don't have any left-over egg then use 3 tbsp milk.

For a vegetarian version, omit garlic sausage or ham and add diced red pepper or sliced mushrooms. Use vegetarian Cheddar.

4oz (100g) self-raising flour
1oz (25g) margarine
1 egg

TOPPING
3 tbsp tomato ketchup
1/4 tsp dried marjoram

2oz (50g)
sliced garlic sausage or ham
3oz (75g) Cheddar cheese
2 lettuce leaves
2 tomatoes

1 Preheat the oven to 425°F, 220°C, Gas 7. Lightly grease a 7in (18.5cm) shallow square tin with margarine.

2 Put flour into a bowl with a pinch of salt. Add margarine, cut into small pieces and rub in until mixture resembles fine crumbs.

3 Gradually add beaten egg and mix to a soft dough. Knead lightly and press into base of tin.

4 Spread ketchup over the top and sprinkle with marjoram. Peel rind away from garlic sausage if using, dice sausage or ham and sprinkle evenly over ketchup. Grate cheese and sprinkle over pizza.

5 Cook for 20 minutes until topping is golden brown.

6 Cut into fingers and remove from tin. Arrange on serving plates with lettuce and tomatoes cut into wedges.

Stuffed marrow

	SAUCE
1 small onion	¹/₂ oz (15g) margarine
4oz (100g) lean minced beef	¹/₂ oz (15g) plain flour
4oz (100g) button mushrooms	¹/₄ pt (150ml) semi-skimmed milk
1 garlic clove, crushed	
¹/₄ tsp ground cinnamon	pinch grated nutmeg
3 tbsp tomato ketchup	1 tbsp Parmesan cheese or breadcrumbs
¹/₄ pt (150ml) beef stock	
¹/₂ small marrow about 1lb (450g)	

COST ££

Buy small quantities of mince from the butcher or divide up supermarket packs into plastic bags and freeze the remainder.

Save unused half marrow for Marrow ratatouille.

1 Preheat oven to 400°F, 200°C, Gas 6. Finely chop onion and put into a small saucepan with mince. Dry fry over a low heat, stirring occasionally, until evenly browned.

2 Slice mushrooms and add to pan with garlic, cinnamon, ketchup, stock and seasoning. Bring to the boil, stirring, and simmer uncovered for 15 minutes.

3 Meanwhile, trim end from marrow, cut into 4 thick slices. Cut out central core and seeds with a small round pastry cutter or knife.

4 Cook marrow in a saucepan of boiling, lightly salted water for 5 minutes. Drain, rinse with cold water and drain again.

5 To make sauce: melt margarine in a small saucepan. Stir in flour then gradually add milk and bring to the boil, stirring until thickened and smooth. Add nutmeg and seasoning.

6 Put marrow slices in a shallow ovenproof dish. Spoon mince mixture into centre of each and pile remainder on top of marrow slices. Pour sauce over the top and sprinkle with Parmesan or breadcrumbs.

7 Cook just below centre of the oven for 30 minutes until golden brown. Transfer to serving plates and serve immediately.

MONDAY PUDDING

Plum clafouti

COST £

Could use canned apricots.

Mix batter in a food processor or in a liquidiser or with an electric beater if preferred.

Make sure fruit is hot before adding batter or it won't rise.

½ oz (15g) margarine
8oz (225g) plums
1½ oz (40g) plain flour
1oz (25g) icing sugar
1 egg

¼ pt (150ml) semi-skimmed milk
few drops vanilla essence

TO DECORATE
sifted icing sugar

1 Lightly grease a 1¼ pt (750ml) pie dish with a little of the margarine and heat in the oven at 400°F, 200°C, Gas 6 on shelf above the stuffed marrow for 5 minutes.

2 Halve plums, discard stones and slice thickly.

3 Add plums to pie dish and cook for 5 minutes. Meanwhile, mix all remaining ingredients, including remaining margarine, together in a bowl until smooth.

4 Pour this batter over hot fruit and return to the oven for 30 minutes until well risen and golden. Dust with icing sugar and serve warm.

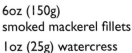

Mackerel and watercress pâté

6oz (150g)
smoked mackerel fillets

1oz (25g) watercress

4oz (100g)
low-fat soft cheese

2tsp lemon juice

wholemeal toast

4 sticks celery

COST £ £

Quick to make.

1 Peel skin away from mackerel using a knife and fork. Break fish into pieces.

2 Pick over watercress and trim stalks. If you have a food processor, put mackerel, watercress, soft cheese and lemon juice into processor bowl. Add seasoning and mix until smooth. If not, mash mackerel with a fork. Finely chop watercress and mix together with soft cheese and lemon juice in a bowl.

Freezes for up to one month. Stir well when thawed.

3 Spoon into 2 ramekin dishes and serve with hot toast and celery sticks.

Stir-fried pork with egg fried rice

8oz (225g)
boneless pork chump chop

4 carrots

2 sticks celery

6oz (150g) green cabbage

4oz (100g) long grain rice

4tsp sunflower oil

1 garlic clove, crushed

2tbsp tomato ketchup

2tbsp soy sauce

2tbsp sherry or stock

1/4 tsp ground ginger

1 egg

COST £ £

Quick to prepare and cook.

Makes a little meat go a long way.

Vary veg depending on what you have. Could add courgettes or broccoli.

1 Trim fat off chop and then cut meat into thin crossways slices. Thinly slice carrots and celery. Finely shred cabbage discarding woody core.

2 Cook rice in a saucepan of boiling, lightly salted water for 10 minutes until just tender.

3 Meanwhile, heat 3tsp oil in a wok or large frying pan. Add pork and carrots and stir fry for 7 minutes.

4 Add celery, cabbage and garlic and stir fry for 5 minutes.

5 Add ketchup, soy sauce, sherry or stock and ginger and mix together. Cook for 1 minute.

6 Drain rice, rinse with hot water and drain again. Dry pan; heat remaining teaspoon of oil, add rice and beaten egg and cook, stirring until egg looks 'scrambled'.

7 Spoon rice and pork stir fry on to plates and serve immediately.

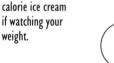

TUESDAY PUDDING

Banana and kiwi sundae

COST £

Choose reduced-calorie ice cream if watching your weight.

1 kiwi fruit   2 scoops vanilla ice cream
1 banana

1 Peel and roughly chop kiwi fruit. Liquidise or process to a smooth purée. Press through a sieve and discard seeds.

2 Slice banana and arrange in two glass dishes with ice cream. Spoon kiwi purée over and serve immediately.

Quick to make.

Ploughman's salad

4 tomatoes

¹/₄ small onion

1 tbsp sunflower oil

1 tsp wine vinegar

¹/₂ tsp coarse grain mustard

2oz (50g) watercress

4oz (100g) red Leicester or Cheddar cheese

¹/₂ small dessert apple, optional

1 small French bread stick

COST ££

Quick to make.

1 Thinly slice tomatoes and onion. Mix oil, vinegar, mustard and seasoning together in a small bowl. Add tomato and onion and toss in dressing.

2 Pick over watercress and break into small sprigs discarding long stalks.

3 Derind and thinly slice cheese. Core and thinly slice apple if using.

As there is fibre in the tomatoes and apple, you can use a white bread stick, but look for a brown one as the healthier choice.

4 Spoon tomato, onion and dressing on to two serving plates. Arrange watercress sprigs, cheese, and apple if using, attractively on top. Serve with slices of French bread.

Store remaining watercress in blown up bag in the fridge.

Make just before serving or watercress will wilt.

Humble pie

1 small onion
1 dessert apple
8oz (225g) herby pork sausages
¹/₂ tsp dried sage

PASTRY
4oz (100g) wholemeal flour
2oz (50g) margarine

1 egg to glaze
2tsp sesame seeds, optional

SALAD
1tbsp sunflower oil
1tsp wine vinegar
¹/₂ tsp coarse grain mustard
¹/₂ lettuce
¹/₄ cucumber

1 Preheat oven to 400°F, 200°C, Gas 6. Finely chop onion. Quarter, core and finely chop apple.

2 Slit sausage skins lengthways and peel off. Mix sausagemeat, onion, apple, sage and seasoning together in a bowl.

3 To make pastry: put flour and a pinch of salt into a bowl. Add margarine, cut into pieces and rub in with fingertips until mixture resembles fine crumbs.

4 Add 5–6tsp cold water and mix to a soft dough. Knead pastry lightly and roll out on a floured surface to a rectangle 8 x 12in (20 x 30cm).

5 Spread sausagemeat mixture over top half of pastry, pressing into an even layer, leaving a ¹/₂in (1cm) border of pastry.

6 Brush pastry edges with beaten egg. Fold bottom half of pastry up to enclose filling, rather like a large Cornish pasty, and press edges together well to seal. Trim pastry edges to neaten.

7 Slide a baking sheet under pie. Slash top with a knife. Brush with egg and sprinkle with sesame seeds if using.

8 Cook for 30 minutes until browned. Meanwhile make salad. Mix oil, vinegar, mustard and seasoning in the base of a salad bowl. Wash and dry lettuce and cucumber. Break leaves into bite-sized pieces and slice cucumber. Toss in dressing.

9 Cut pie into thick slices and serve with salad.

PUDDING WEDNESDAY

Baked nectarines

2 ripe nectarines
1oz (25g) macaroon biscuits

2tbsp apricot jam or marmalade
1tbsp sherry or water

COST £

1 Halve nectarines and discard stones. Put fruits, cut side uppermost, in a shallow ovenproof dish.

Quick to make.

2 Crush macaroons with your fingertips and mix in a small bowl with the jam or marmalade and sherry or water.

3 Spoon mixture on to nectarines and cook at 400° F, 200° C, Gas 6 on shelf above Humble pie for 15 minutes until hot.

Could buy 1 large macaroon from baker.

Could use 4 halved plums instead.

Nutty Scotch eggs

COST ££

Lower in fat than traditional version.

Suitable for a vegetarian.

Store cupboard ingredients.

If you have difficulty in moulding mixture around egg, mix in a little more milk.

2 hardboiled eggs
1/2 small onion
1 tbsp sunflower oil
2 slices wholemeal bread
2oz (50g) unblanched almonds
1/2 tsp paprika

1 tbsp semi-skimmed milk
1 tbsp sesame seeds

CARROT SALAD

3 carrots
2 sticks celery
2 tbsp reduced-calorie mayonnaise

1 Preheat oven to 400°F, 200°C, Gas 6. Rinse eggs with cold water if still hot. Shell and set aside.

2 Finely chop onion. Heat oil in a small frying pan and fry onion until soft.

3 Break bread into pieces, roughly chop almonds. Place both in food processor or liquidiser and blend until finely chopped. Add fried onion, paprika, milk and seasoning and mix together.

4 Take half the nut mixture and flatten slightly on a chopping board until a little larger than one of the eggs. Mould nut mixture all around egg using palm of your hand. Repeat with remaining nut mixture and egg.

5 Sprinkle sesame seeds over nut mixture. Roll eggs at the same time until evenly coated in seeds.

6 Place on a small baking sheet and cook for 25 minutes. Cool.

7 Meanwhile, grate carrots coarsely and slice celery thinly. Put into a small bowl, add mayonnaise and seasoning and mix together. Serve with the eggs.

Mushroom quiche

4oz (100g) wholemeal flour

2oz (50g) margarine

4oz (100g) mushrooms

1tbsp sunflower oil

2 eggs

7fl oz (210ml) semi-skimmed milk

3oz (75g) red Leicester or Cheddar cheese

BEAN SALAD

2oz (50g) frozen sweetcorn

1 tomato

1tbsp sunflower oil

1tsp wine vinegar

$1/2$ tsp coarse grain mustard

10oz (283g) can broad beans

2tbsp fresh or frozen chopped chives or parsley, optional

COST ££

Grow parsley, chives or mint in flowerpots on the window sill; this is much cheaper than buying packets.

Cook quiche at same time as Scotch eggs and serve cold.

Make pastry with an electric mixer or food processor to save time.

1 Preheat oven to 400°F, 200°C, Gas 6. Put flour and a pinch of salt into a bowl. Add margarine cut into small pieces and rub in with fingertips until mixture resembles fine crumbs.

2 Add 5–6tsp water and mix to a smooth dough. Knead lightly and roll out on a floured surface until a little larger than a 7in (18.5cm) flan tin.

3 Lift pastry over the rolling pin and place in greased flan tin. Press into base and sides of tin and trim top.

4 Slice mushrooms and fry in oil for 3 minutes. Cool slightly.

5 Mix eggs, milk and seasoning together. Grate cheese, stir into egg mixture then pour into flan tin.

6 Drain mushrooms well and add to flan. Cook for 30 minutes until golden brown and well set.

7 Meanwhile, cook sweetcorn in a small saucepan of boiling water for 3 minutes. Drain, rinse with cold water and drain again. Dice tomato.

8 Mix oil, vinegar, mustard and seasoning together in a bowl. Add sweetcorn, tomato, drained broad beans and parsley or chives, if using. Mix together and serve with wedges of quiche.

THURSDAY PUDDING

Tangy fruit salad

COST £

Quick to prepare.

Virtually fat free. Low in calories, high in vitamin C.

I banana	2oz (50g) strawberries,
I kiwi fruit	optional
2 oranges	2tbsp natural yogurt

1 Thickly slice banana. Peel and slice kiwi fruit. Hull and slice strawberries, if using.

2 Cut top and bottom off each orange with a small serrated knife. Stand oranges on a chopping board and cut remaining peel and pith away beginning at the top and cutting down towards base.

3 Hold one orange over a serving dish and cut into segments. Squeeze juice from membrane. Repeat with remaining orange. Add other fruits to dish and toss together. Serve with natural yogurt.

Minted pea soup

1 small onion
1oz (25g) margarine
8oz (225g) frozen peas
2tsp fresh chopped mint
or ¹/₄ tsp dried
¹/₂ pt (300ml) chicken stock
6tbsp semi-skimmed milk

CROÛTONS
2 slices wholemeal bread
¹/₂ oz (15g) margarine
2tbsp sunflower oil

COST £

Peas are surprisingly high in fibre.

1 Finely chop onion. Heat margarine in a saucepan, add onion and fry for 5 minutes, stirring occasionally until softened but not browned.

2 Add peas, mint, stock and seasoning. Bring to the boil, cover and simmer for 10 minutes.

3 Cool slightly then process or liquidise until smooth. Return to pan with milk and reheat.

4 To make croûtons: dice bread. Heat margarine and oil in a frying pan. Add bread and fry, stirring frequently until evenly browned. Drain on kitchen paper.

5 Ladle soup into serving bowls, sprinkle with a few croûtons and serve remainder separately.

When there is room in the oven, bake diced bread on a greased baking sheet, turning occasionally for low-fat croûtons. Freeze in a plastic box.

Could use a mixture of yogurt and milk. Mix yogurt with ¹/₂ tsp cornflour before adding to soup to prevent it curdling.

Store cupboard ingredients.

Kedgeree

COST £££

If you want to use white rice, add fish to fried rice, reduce water to ½pt (300ml) and cook for 10–12 minutes.

I small onion
1oz (25g) margarine
6oz (150g) easy-cook brown rice
½tsp turmeric
I bay leaf
I egg
12oz (325g) frozen smoked haddock
2oz (50g) frozen peas

1 Finely chop onion. Heat margarine in a deep frying pan. Add onion and fry for 5 minutes, stirring occasionally until softened but not browned.

2 Add rice and cook for 2 minutes. Add ¾pt (450ml) water, turmeric, bay leaf and seasoning. Bring to the boil, reduce heat, cover and simmer for 25 minutes.

3 Hardboil egg in a small saucepan of boiling water for 10 minutes. Drain, rinse in cold water.

4 Peel skin away from frozen fish. Stir rice and add more water if needed, then add haddock and peas. Cover pan and cook for 10 minutes or until fish flakes easily when pressed with a knife.

5 Peel and cut egg into wedges. Break fish into pieces with a wooden spoon. Add egg and serve immediately.

Summer pudding

8oz (225g) mixed strawberries and blackcurrants

1oz (25g) caster sugar

6 thin slices white bread

COST £

1 Hull strawberries and remove stems from blackcurrants. Put fruit and sugar into a saucepan with 6tbsp water. Cook gently for 5 minutes until just soft.

2 Drain juice into a shallow dish and reserve fruit.

3 Trim crusts from bread. Cut 2 small rounds, dip one side of each into fruit juice and place juice side downwards in base of 2 cups.

4 Cut remaining bread into thin strips, dip one side of each into juice and arrange slightly overlapping, juice side outwards, around sides of cups.

5 Spoon in fruit, trim bread level with top of cups and use trimmings to cover fruit.

6 Cover each cup with a saucer and weight down. Chill in fridge for 4–5 hours or overnight.

7 Loosen edge of bread and turn puddings out on to 2 small serving plates. Serve immediately.

Shop around for bargain fruit buys at your pick-your-own farm or local market.

Fat free.

Can make the day before and keep in fridge.

Marrow ratatouille

COST £

Use courgettes when marrow is out of season.

Could sprinkle with grated cheese to serve.

I small onion
3 carrots
¹/₂ small marrow about Ilb (450g)
I tbsp sunflower oil
I garlic clove, crushed

8oz (227g) can tomatoes
¹/₂ tsp dried thyme
¹/₂ tsp granulated sugar
wholemeal bread

1 Thinly slice onion and carrots.

2 Halve marrow lengthways then cut into thick slices discarding end. Cut away central core and seeds and cut remaining flesh into chunky pieces.

3 Heat oil in a saucepan, add onion and carrots and fry for 5 minutes, stirring occasionally.

4 Add marrow and garlic and cook for 3 minutes.

5 Add tomatoes, thyme, sugar and seasoning. Bring to the boil, breaking up tomatoes with a spoon. Cover and simmer for 15 minutes until marrow is tender.

6 Spoon ratatouille into dishes and serve with wholemeal bread.

Tandoori-style chicken

4 chicken drumsticks

6oz (150g) carton natural yogurt

1tsp hot curry paste or powder

1tsp paprika

¼ tsp turmeric

8oz (225g) new potatoes

CELERY SALAD

3 sticks celery

¼ cucumber

1tsp wine vinegar

pinch granulated sugar

2tsp fresh chopped mint or ¼tsp dried

COST ££

Low-fat and low in calories.

Can cook chicken on barbecue, too.

1 Peel skin away from chicken drumsticks and slash meat 2 or 3 times with a small knife.

2 Put yogurt and spices in a small bowl and mix together. Add drumsticks, one at a time and spoon yogurt mixture over. Cover and chill for 2–3 hours.

3 Remove chicken from fridge and allow to come to room temperature. Preheat oven to 350° F, 180° C, Gas 4.

4 Drain chicken and arrange on a rack set over a small roasting tin. Pour a little water into base of tin so it is completely covered, then cook chicken for 45 minutes. To test it is thoroughly done, insert a skewer into thickest part of drumsticks, juices should run clear.

5 Scrub potatoes, halve any large ones and cook in boiling, lightly salted water for 20 minutes. Slice celery and dice cucumber. Put celery and cucumber in a small bowl, add vinegar, sugar, mint and seasoning and toss together.

6 Arrange chicken on serving plates with drained potatoes and celery salad.

Orange sorbet

Fat free.

Best made day before
required.

Could serve with
sliced strawberries.

Store cupboard
ingredients.

2 oranges   3oz (75g) granulated sugar

1 Finely grate orange rind and squeeze juice.

2 Put orange rind, sugar and ½ pt (300ml) water into a saucepan and heat gently until sugar has dissolved. Bring to boil and boil rapidly for 5 minutes.

3 Remove from heat, cool slightly and stir in orange juice. Pour into a shallow plastic container and leave to cool.

4 Freeze for 3–4 hours until mushy then beat with a fork or process until smooth. Freeze for 4–5 hours or overnight until solid.

5 Remove from freezer 15 minutes before serving so sorbet can soften slightly. Scoop into glass dishes and serve immediately.

SHOPPING LIST

FRUIT AND VEGETABLES

11 small onions
1¾ lb (800g) carrots
2lb (900g) potatoes
1 small swede
1¼ lb (550g) parsnips
1 leek
6 tomatoes

4oz (100g)
button mushrooms
1 round lettuce
½ cucumber
2 sticks celery, optional
8oz (225g) Brussels
sprouts

3 lemons
1 orange
1 grapefruit
1 kiwi fruit
2 cooking apples
12oz (325g) plums

DAIRY PRODUCE

11½oz (315g) margarine
6 eggs

8oz (225g)
Cheddar cheese

2¼pt (1.25 litre)
semi-skimmed milk

FRESH MEAT AND FISH

12oz (325g)
hoki fish fillet
6 rashers streaky bacon

2 boneless pork
shoulder steaks
4oz (100g) wafer thin
sliced ham

8oz (225g)
herby pork
chipolata sausages

FROZEN FOODS

12oz (325g) lambs' liver
1lb (450g)
neck of (stewing) lamb

1 rack of lamb
2oz (50g) sweetcorn
2oz (50g) peas

5tbsp chopped parsley
vanilla ice cream,
optional

CANS AND DRY GOODS

2 × 14oz (397g)
cans tomatoes
15.2oz (432g) can
cannellini beans

15.2oz (432g) can
red kidney beans
15.2oz (432g) can
chick peas

4.32oz (120g) can
sardines in brine
14½oz (411g) can
apricot halves in
natural juice

tumn

15oz (425g) can
low-fat custard

1½oz (40g) vegetable suet

8oz (225g) tagliatelle

4oz (100g) continental
green lentils

2 trifle sponges

4oz (100g)
long grain brown rice

9oz (250g) packet
mixed dried fruit salad

4oz (100g) All-Bran cereal

7oz (200g)
self-raising flour

8oz (225g) golden syrup

5oz (125g)
soft light brown sugar

1oz (25g)
desiccated coconut

10oz (275g) raisins

BREAD

1 Granary loaf

3 pitta breads

STORE CUPBOARD

12oz (325g) plain flour

1oz (25g)
medium oatmeal

1oz (25g) porridge oats

1tbsp pearl barley,
optional

2oz (50g) pudding rice

2oz (50g) red lentils

3tbsp lemon juice

11 tbsp sunflower oil

4 garlic cloves

3 chicken stock cubes

2 lamb stock cubes

2 beef stock cubes

1 vegetable stock cube

3½ tsp coarse
grain mustard

2 cocktail gherkins,
optional

2tbsp grated Parmesan,
optional

1tbsp reduced-calorie
mayonnaise

1tbsp tomato purée

1tbsp black treacle

5oz (125g) caster sugar

5tbsp clear honey

2oz (50g) stoned dates
or sultanas

2tsp glacé ginger

2tbsp sherry, optional

HERBS AND SPICES

1tsp curry paste or
curry powder

½ tsp turmeric

¼ tsp paprika

1tsp dried marjoram

¼ tsp dried thyme

2½ tsp dried sage

¼ tsp dried mint

½ tsp ground cumin

½ tsp ground coriander

4 bay leaves

4 cloves

¼ tsp ground nutmeg

½ tsp ground cinnamon

Roast rack of lamb with honey and mint

COST £ £

Shop around as lamb prices vary considerably.

Sprinkle lamb with 2tsp chopped mint if using fresh from the garden.

Add a little dry sherry or wine to the gravy, if you have it.

I rack of frozen New Zealand lamb, defrosted

I tbsp clear honey

¹/₄ tsp dried mint

I tbsp frozen chopped parsley, optional

I tbsp plain flour

¹/₄ pt (150ml) lamb or vegetable stock

1 Preheat oven to 350°F, 180°C, Gas 4. Rinse lamb with cold water, dry with kitchen paper and put, fat uppermost, in a small roasting tin. Sprinkle seasoning over fat.

2 Roast on shelf just above centre of oven (with Potatoes boulangères) for 50 minutes for medium done and 1 hour for well done.

3 Ten minutes before the end of cooking, spoon honey over lamb fat and sprinkle with mint. Add 4tbsp water to roasting tin and return to the oven, until browned.

4 Transfer lamb to a serving plate and sprinkle with parsley. Stir flour into roasting tin and cook for 1 minute. Stir in stock and bring to the boil, stirring continuously. Strain into a gravy boat.

5 Cut lamb between bones and arrange on plates. Serve with Potatoes boulangères, parsnip purée and steamed sprouts (see following recipes).

■ **Frozen lamb is very lean. If using fresh, trim fat to the minimum before cooking.**

Potatoes boulangères

1lb (450g) potatoes
½ small onion
½oz (15g) margarine

¼pt (150ml)
hot lamb or chicken stock
pinch grated nutmeg

COST £

Use a processor for
evenly sliced potatoes.

1 Preheat oven to 350°F, 180°C, Gas 4. Thinly slice
potatoes and onion. Layer in a small ovenproof dish,
seasoning each layer.

2 Pour stock over and dot top layer of potatoes with
margarine. Sprinkle with nutmeg and cook on shelf just
above centre of oven for 1½ hours. Add lamb after first
30 minutes.

Store cupboard
ingredients.

Parsnip purée and steamed sprouts

COST £

12oz (325g) parsnips
4oz (100g) Brussels sprouts

½oz (15g) margarine

1 Dice parsnips and cook in a saucepan of boiling,
lightly salted water for 20 minutes.

2 Meanwhile trim and halve sprouts. Steam above
parsnips for 10 minutes.

3 Drain parsnips and mash with margarine and pepper
until smooth. Spoon vegetables into separate serving
dishes and serve with the lamb.

Reheat parsnips in
their serving dish in
the microwave if you
have one, but check
dish does not have a
metallic decoration.

SUNDAY PUDDING

Rice pudding

COST £

Quick to prepare.

Warming the milk
helps to reduce
cooking time.

Don't be tempted to
use long grain rice, it
doesn't give the same
result.

Store cupboard
ingredients.

Can use brown and
white pudding rice or
all brown for a
healthier alternative.

2oz (50g) pudding rice
1oz (25g) caster sugar
1pt (600ml)
semi-skimmed milk

½oz (15g) margarine
pinch grated nutmeg

1 Put rice and sugar in the base of a shallow ovenproof dish.

2 Bring milk just to the boil in a small saucepan. Pour over rice, dot with margarine and sprinkle with nutmeg.

3 Cook at 350°F, 180°C, Gas 4 on shelf below lamb for 1¼–1½ hours until browned and rice is tender.

All-Bran and raisin tea loaf

4oz (100g) All-Bran

5oz (125g)
soft light brown sugar

10oz (275g) raisins

½pt (300ml) cold tea

4oz (100g) self-raising
flour

COST £

High fibre.

1 Preheat oven to 350°F, 180°C, Gas 4. Grease and base line a 2lb (900g) loaf tin.

2 Put All-Bran, sugar and raisins in a bowl. Pour over tea and leave to soak for 30 minutes.

Save left-over cold tea!

3 Stir in flour and mix well. Spoon into tin and level surface. Cook for 1 hour or until a skewer inserted into centre of cake comes out cleanly.

4 Cool slightly, loosen edges of cake and turn out on to a wire rack. Cut into slices when cool. Serve buttered if liked.

Store cupboard
ingredients.

■ **If the skewer comes out of the cake looking sticky then return cake to the oven and check again 10 minutes later.**

■ **Store the cake in a biscuit tin or in a plastic bag for up to 1 week.**

Cheese and oatmeal tart

COST ££

Buy cheese when on special offer, grate and freeze.

Don't have any oatmeal? Use an extra 1oz (25g) of plain flour.

PASTRY
3oz (75g) plain flour
1oz (25g) medium oatmeal
2oz (50g) margarine

FILLING
2 small onions
1tbsp sunflower oil
3oz (75g) Cheddar cheese

2 egg yolks (save whites for Hot apricot trifle)
1 whole egg
7fl oz (210ml) semi-skimmed milk
pinch paprika

SALAD
¼ cucumber
2 tomatoes

1 Preheat the oven to 400°F, 200°C, Gas 6. Put flour, oatmeal and seasoning into a bowl. Add margarine, cut into pieces and rub in with fingertips or an electric mixer until mixture resembles fine crumbs.

2 Stir in 1tbsp water and mix to a smooth, slightly soft dough. Knead and roll out on a lightly floured surface.

3 Lift pastry over a rolling pin and use to line a greased 7in (18.5cm) flan tin or sponge tin. Trim top.

4 To make filling: thinly slice onions. Heat oil in a frying pan, add onions and fry for 5 minutes until lightly browned.

5 Grate cheese. Spoon half the onions into the tin, sprinkle with half the cheese and repeat. Put egg yolks, whole egg, milk and seasoning in a small bowl and mix with a fork. Pour into tin. Sprinkle with a little paprika and cook for 30–35 minutes until set.

6 Dice cucumber and tomatoes, season and mix together. Serve with warm tart.

Ossobuco pork

1 tbsp sunflower oil

2 boneless pork
shoulder steaks

1 small onion

2 carrots

2 sticks celery, optional

1 tbsp plain flour

1 garlic clove, crushed

¹/₄ tsp dried thyme

14oz (397g) can tomatoes

pinch sugar

1 lemon

4oz (100g) long grain
brown rice

2oz (50g) frozen peas

1 tbsp frozen
chopped parsley, optional

COST ££

Can use spare rib
pork chops too, trim
off fat before using.

Double up recipe if
entertaining.

Freeze up to 3
months in a plastic
box.

1 Preheat the oven to 350° F, 180° C, Gas 4. Heat the oil
in a flame-proof casserole, add pork and fry until
browned on both sides.

2 Meanwhile, chop onion, dice carrots and celery,
if using.

3 Remove pork from casserole, add vegetables and fry
for 5 minutes, stirring occasionally, until softened.

4 Stir in flour. Add garlic, thyme, tomatoes, sugar and
seasoning. Grate lemon, reserve rind and squeeze juice.
Stir juice into casserole and add meat.

5 Bring pork mixture to the boil, cover and transfer to
the oven for 1¹/₄ hours.

6 Half an hour before serving, cook rice in a saucepan
of boiling, lightly salted water for 25 minutes. Add peas
and cook for 5 minutes more. Drain.

7 Spoon pork on to serving plates, sprinkle with
reserved lemon rind and a little parsley, if using. Serve
with rice and peas.

■ **If using celery, save the leaves for garnish. Store in a blown up plastic bag
in the fridge.**

MONDAY PUDDING

Baked apples

COST £

Look out for glacé ginger, it's much cheaper than crystallised or stem ginger.

Slit apples before cooking so they don't burst in the oven.

Use a pinch of ground ginger in place of glacé ginger.

2 medium-sized cooking apples

2oz (50g) stoned dates or sultanas

2tsp glacé ginger

2tbsp clear honey

¹/₂ x 15oz (425g) can low-fat custard (save remaining half for Hot apricot trifle)

1 Wash apples, core and make a slit around the waist of each. Put into a shallow ovenproof dish.

2 Chop dates, if using, and put dates or sultanas into a small bowl with the ginger and honey. Mix together and spoon into apples. Spoon 2tbsp water into base of dish.

3 Cook alongside the Ossobuco pork at 350°F, 180°C, Gas 4 for 1 hour.

4 Reserving half the can of custard for the following day, warm remainder in a small saucepan or pour into a bowl and microwave on Full Power (100%) for 1¹/₂ minutes.

5 Transfer apple mixture to serving bowls and spoon custard around.

Curried lentil and vegetable soup

I small onion	¹/₂ tsp turmeric
I carrot	I tsp hot curry paste or powder
I potato	
I parsnip	2oz (50g) red lentils
I tbsp sunflower oil	I ¹/₂ pt (900ml) chicken stock

COST £

I Finely chop onion, dice carrot, potato and parsnip.

2 Heat oil in a saucepan, add vegetables and fry, stirring for 5 minutes until softened.

3 Add turmeric and curry paste or powder and cook for 1 minute. Add lentils, stock and seasoning.

4 Bring to the boil, stirring. Reduce heat, cover and simmer for 40 minutes until lentils are soft.

5 Ladle into soup bowls and serve with Granary bread.

Freeze for up to 6 months.

Store cupboard ingredients.

Vary the vegetables depending on what you have in your vegetable rack.

■ **Red lentils and the large green continental lentils don't need soaking before use and are a good source of protein and fibre.**

Pan-fried liver and bacon

COST ££

Liver and kidneys are high in iron.

If you don't have a steamer, use a metal colander over a saucepan and cover with a large saucepan lid.

½ swede

2 potatoes

1 small onion

1oz (25g) margarine

1 tbsp sunflower oil

2 rashers streaky bacon

12oz (325g) packet frozen lambs' livers, defrosted

1 leek

2oz (50g) button mushrooms, optional

1 tbsp plain flour

¼ pt (150ml) beef stock

½ tsp coarse grain mustard

2tsp grated orange rind (reserve remaining orange for Three-fruit salad)

1 tbsp semi-skimmed milk

1 Peel and dice swede and potatoes. Cook in a saucepan of boiling, lightly salted water for 15 minutes until soft.

2 Slice onion. Heat half the margarine with the oil in a frying pan, add onion and fry for 5 minutes, stirring occasionally until softened.

3 Meanwhile, derind and chop bacon. Put liver into a colander or sieve, rinse well with cold water. Drain and cut into strips. Slice mushrooms, if using.

4 Slit leek lengthways, rinse with cold water, drain and slice thickly.

5 Add bacon, liver and mushrooms to onion and fry over a high heat, stirring constantly for 3 minutes.

6 Steam leek over swede and potatoes for 8 minutes until tender.

7 Stir flour into liver mixture, then add stock, mustard and seasoning. Bring to the boil and simmer for 8 minutes until tender. Sprinkle with orange rind.

8 Drain swede and potato and mash with remaining margarine, milk and pepper. Spoon on to serving plates and serve with leeks and liver.

Hot apricot trifle

2 trifle sponges

2tbsp sherry or orange juice

14¹/₂ oz (411g) can apricot halves

¹/₂ x 15oz (425g) can low-fat custard

2 egg whites (reserved from Cheese and oatmeal tart) or equivalent dried egg white

2oz (50g) caster sugar

COST £ £

Quick to make.

1 Preheat oven to 325° F, 160° C, Gas 3. Crumble trifle sponges into the base of two single-serving pie dishes or large ramekin dishes. Spoon sherry or orange juice over each.

Buy fresh fruits, eg plums, strawberries, when cheap and use in preference to canned fruit.

2 Drain and slice apricots. Divide between dishes. Spoon custard over the top.

3 Put egg whites into a bowl and whisk until stiff, moist-looking peaks (or follow packet directions if using dried egg white). Gradually whisk in sugar, 1tsp at a time and continue whisking for a minute or two until meringue is thick and glossy.

Can do steps 1 and 2 in advance. Make and cook meringue just before eating main course.

4 Spoon into dishes over custard and swirl the top with the back of a spoon. Cook for 10–12 minutes until meringue is golden. Serve warm.

Don't forget to use reserved custard and egg whites from day before.

■ **Always make sure you have a dry, grease-free bowl when whisking egg whites or they won't whip up.**

■ **Ovens vary in temperature so check half way through cooking to make sure meringue isn't overbrowning.**

Carbonara

COST £

Quick to make.

Vary types of pasta, eg spaghetti, pasta twists or shells.

For a vegetarian version, omit bacon and fry sliced courgettes with the mushrooms in a little oil.

Store cupboard ingredients.

4oz (100g) tagliatelle
4 rashers streaky bacon
2oz (50g) button mushrooms
1oz (25g) margarine
1 egg
2tbsp semi-skimmed milk
2tbsp grated Parmesan or Cheddar cheese

1 Cook pasta in a large saucepan of boiling, lightly salted water for 10 minutes until pasta is just tender.

2 Meanwhile, derind and chop bacon, wipe and slice mushrooms.

3 Drain pasta and rinse with boiling water.

4 Dry pan and add bacon and mushrooms. Cook over a gentle heat until fat begins to run from bacon then increase heat and fry, stirring, until bacon is golden.

5 Add margarine and when just melting, return pasta to pan. Beat egg, milk and plenty of black pepper together. Add to pan and cook over a gentle heat, stirring and turning pasta until evenly coated and egg is set. Spoon into bowls and sprinkle with cheese.

Irish stew

1 small onion	¼ pt (450ml) lamb stock
½ small swede	2tsp dried sage
1 carrot	1tbsp pearl barley, optional
1 small parsnip	
1lb (450g) frozen neck (stewing) lamb, defrosted	**DUMPLINGS**
	3oz (75g) self-raising flour
1tbsp sunflower oil	1½oz (40g) suet
	½tsp dried sage

You'll find bargain boxes of root veg in the market at packing up time.

1 Preheat the oven to 325°F, 160°C, Gas 3. Finely chop onion. Dice swede, carrot and parsnip. Trim fat off lamb.

2 Heat the oil in a flame proof casserole, add the vegetables and fry for 5 minutes, stirring until softened.

3 Add lamb with stock, sage, pearl barley, if using, and seasoning. Bring to the boil, cover and transfer to the oven. Cook for 1½ hours.

Can make stew the day before. Skim off fat when cold. Reheat thoroughly, add dumplings, cover and cook on hob for 15 minutes.

4 Transfer lamb to a plate and using a sharp knife and fork, cut meat away from bones. Add to casserole and return to the oven.

5 Put dumpling ingredients and seasoning into a bowl. Add 3–4tbsp water and mix to a soft dough. Shape into small balls with lightly floured hands and add to hot stew.

Could use a slow cooker, follow manufacturer's booklet for timings.

6 Cover stew again and return to the oven for 30 minutes until dumplings are well risen.

7 Spoon into soup bowls and serve.

Spiced fruit compôte

COST £

High fibre.

If you forget to soak the fruit, cover with boiling water, leave for 30–40 minutes before cooking. Cook for 20 minutes on the hob.

9oz (250g) packet mixed dried fruit salad

1 tbsp clear honey

4 cloves

¹/₂ tsp ground cinnamon

vanilla ice cream, optional

1 Put all ingredients into an ovenproof casserole with ¹/₂ pt (300ml) water and leave to soak overnight or for at least 4 hours.

2 Stir mixture and cover with lid or foil. Cook alongside the Irish stew at 325° F, 160° C, Gas 3 for 1¹/₄ hours.

3 Spoon into bowls and serve warm with ice cream, optional.

Reheat any left-over fruit and serve for breakfast.

Carrot soup

1 small onion
1lb (450g) carrots
1oz (25g) margarine
½ tsp ground cumin
½ tsp ground coriander

1pt (600ml) chicken stock
¼pt (150ml) semi-skimmed milk

TO SERVE
ham and cucumber

COST £

High in vitamin A.

1 Chop onion and carrots. Heat margarine in a saucepan and fry vegetables for 5 minutes, stirring occasionally until softened but not browned.

2 Stir in spices and cook 1 minute. Add stock and seasoning and bring to the boil. Stir well and simmer for 20 minutes until vegetables are soft.

3 Cool slightly then process or liquidise until smooth. Return to pan and stir in milk. Reheat and serve in bowls – with a ham and cucumber sandwich.

Don't have a processor or liquidiser? Drain off liquid after cooking vegetables, mash carrots until smooth and return to pan with liquid.

Store cupboard ingredients.

Freezes for up to 6 months.

■ For different flavours, substitute Jerusalem artichokes, cauliflower or celeriac in place of carrots. Omit spices and add a little crumbled **Stilton** or **Danish blue cheese** at the end of cooking.

Boston baked beans

High fibre.

Can use a slow cooker if you have one.

Could use a small can of red kidney beans and serve with frozen green beans.

Freezes for up to 3 months in a plastic box.

8oz (225g) herby chipolata sausages

2 small onions

2 carrots

1 tbsp plain flour

¹/₂ pt (300ml) beef stock

2tsp coarse grain mustard

1 tbsp tomato purée

1 tbsp black treacle

2 bay leaves

15.2oz (432g) can cannellini beans

15.2oz (432g) can red kidney beans

TO SERVE

Granary bread

1 Preheat the oven to 350° F, 180° C, Gas 4. Squeeze the centre of each sausage, twist and cut into 2 smaller sausages. Prick and fry gently without any oil in a flame-proof casserole.

2 Finely chop onions, dice carrots and add to sausages. Fry, stirring occasionally, until sausages are evenly browned.

3 Stir in flour, then add the stock, mustard, tomato purée, treacle and bay leaves. Drain beans and add to casserole with plenty of seasoning.

4 Bring to the boil, stirring, then cover and transfer to the oven and cook for 45 minutes.

5 Spoon into soup bowls discarding bay leaves and serve with warm Granary bread.

■ **If you have a pressure cooker you can use dried beans. Pre-soak and cook according to manufacturer's handbook.**

Three-fruit salad

I orange (reserved from
Pan-fried liver and bacon)

I grapefruit

I kiwi fruit

I tbsp clear honey

COST £

Quick to make.

High in vitamin C.
This vitamin is not
stored by the body,
so is required daily.

I Cut a slice off the top and bottom of the orange with a serrated knife and stand orange on chopping board. Cut peel and pith away, beginning at the top and cutting down towards base of the orange.

2 Holding orange over a shallow dish, cut between membranes to release fruit segments. Put into the dish. Squeeze juice from pithy membrane and repeat process with the grapefruit.

3 Peel kiwi fruit and cut into thin crossways slices. Add to orange and grapefruit and drizzle honey over. Mix together and chill until required.

Hummus

COST £

Quick to make.

Could use 1tbsp
bottled lemon juice.

Freeze remaining
pittas, then grill from
frozen.

15.2oz (432g) can chick peas
½ lemon
1–2 garlic cloves, crushed
2tbsp sunflower oil
2tbsp semi-skimmed milk

pinch paprika
2 tomatoes
½ small onion
4 lettuce leaves
3 pitta breads

1 Drain chick peas and put into a food processor or liquidiser. Grate rind of and squeeze juice from lemon, add to chick peas with garlic, oil, milk, paprika and seasoning. Process to a smooth purée.

2 Spoon into 2 ramekin dishes and sprinkle with paprika. Put dishes on plates. Slice tomatoes and onion thinly, tear lettuce into bite-sized pieces, arrange on plates and season.

3 Sprinkle pitta breads with cold water and cook under a hot grill for 2–3 minutes, turning once, until hot and puffy. Cut into strips and arrange on plates with salad.

■ Grate rind from a whole lemon before squeezing for juice, it's almost impossible to grate a squeezed lemon.

Cheesy fish pie

12oz (325g) potatoes	1½oz (40g) margarine
1 egg	1oz (25g) plain flour
12oz (325g) hoki fish fillet	3oz (75g) Cheddar cheese
½pt (300ml) semi-skimmed milk	2oz (50g) frozen sweetcorn
	pinch paprika
2 bay leaves	4oz (100g) Brussels sprouts

COST £££

Hoki is one of the cheapest fish to buy and yet is fished from around Australia and New Zealand! Use coley if you can't obtain it.

1 Scrub and thinly slice potatoes. Cook in saucepan of boiling, lightly salted water for 4–5 minutes until just tender. Drain, rinse with cold water and drain again. Dry pan.

2 Hardboil egg in a small saucepan of boiling water for 10 minutes. Drain, crack shell, rinse with cold water, drain and cool.

Can make earlier in the day. Reheat thoroughly when needed.

3 Cut fish into two pieces and put into dry potato pan. Add milk, bay leaves and seasoning. Bring to boil, then reduce heat, cover and simmer for 10 minutes.

4 Preheat oven to 375°F, 190°C, Gas 5. Lift fish out of pan with a draining spoon. Peel away skin using a knife and fork and break into chunky pieces. Strain milk into a measuring jug discarding bay leaves, and make up to ½pt (300ml) with water.

5 Wash and dry pan. Melt 1oz (25g) margarine then stir in flour. Cook 1 minute then gradually stir in milk and bring to the boil, stirring continuously, until thickened and smooth.

Use dried milk if running low on fresh milk.

6 Grate cheese. Stir in 2oz (50g), with sweetcorn and fish. Shell and chop egg then stir into sauce. Pour into a shallow ovenproof dish. Arrange potatoes overlapping on top, dot remaining margarine over and sprinkle with remaining cheese. Sprinkle with paprika.

7 Cook for 30–35 minutes until browned. Meanwhile, trim and halve Brussels sprouts. Cook in boiling, lightly salted water for 10 minutes to be ready with pie.

8 Drain sprouts and serve with pie.

FRIDAY PUDDING

Plum and coconut crumble

COST **££**

Use rhubarb, gooseberries or greengages when in season.

Make crumble topping with an electric mixer or food processor if you have one.

12oz (325g) plums	1¹/₂ oz (40g) margarine
2oz (50g) caster sugar	1oz (25g) desiccated coconut
3oz (75g) plain flour	vanilla ice cream, optional

1 Halve and stone plums. Put into a shallow ovenproof dish with 1oz (25g) sugar.

2 Put the flour and remaining sugar in a bowl. Add margarine, cut into pieces and then rub in with fingertips until mixture resembles fine crumbs.

3 Stir in coconut and spoon mixture over plums. Cook alongside Cheesy fish pie at 375°F, 190°C, Gas 5 for 30–35 minutes. Serve with ice cream if liked.

Uncooked crumble freezes well in a polybag for up to 3 months.

Sardine toasts

4.23oz (120g) can
sardines in brine

1 tbsp reduced-calorie
mayonnaise

1 tsp lemon juice

2 cocktail gherkins,
optional

2 slices Granary bread

2 tomatoes

1 Drain sardines and mash in a bowl with the
mayonnaise, lemon juice and seasoning.

2 Drain and chop gherkins if using and stir into
sardines.

3 Toast bread on both sides, spread one side with
sardine mixture and cut into triangles. Cut tomatoes
into wedges and arrange on two plates.

COST £

Quick to make.

Include at least one
meal using oily fish
each week.

Always keep a sliced
loaf in the freezer
just in case you can't
get to the shops.

Lentil bolognese

High fibre.

Lentils are a cheap alternative to minced beef and make the recipe suitable for a vegetarian, if using vegetarian Cheddar.

You may need to add a little extra stock towards end of cooking.

Freeze (lentil mixture only) in a polybag for up to 6 months.

Store cupboard ingredients.

I small onion
I carrot
2tbsp sunflower oil
I garlic clove, crushed
4oz (100g) continental green lentils
14oz (397g) can tomatoes
¼pt (150ml) vegetable stock
Itsp dried marjoram
4oz (100g) tagliatelle
½ round lettuce
Itsp lemon juice
3tbsp frozen chopped parsley, optional
Ioz (25g) Cheddar cheese

1 Finely chop onion. Dice carrot. Heat 1tbsp oil in a saucepan and add onion and carrot. Fry for 5 minutes until lightly browned.

2 Stir in garlic, lentils, tomatoes, stock, marjoram and seasoning. Bring to the boil, then cover and simmer for 50 minutes, stirring occasionally, until lentils are soft. Add more stock if needed.

3 Cook pasta in a large saucepan of boiling, lightly salted water for 10–12 minutes until just tender.

4 Separate lettuce leaves, wash and drain then tear into bite-sized pieces. Mix remaining oil, lemon juice, 1tbsp parsley, if using, and seasoning in a salad bowl. Add lettuce and toss together.

5 Drain pasta, rinse with boiling water, drain again and add to lentil mixture with remaining parsley, if using. Toss together and spoon on to serving plates.

6 Grate cheese and sprinkle over bolognese. Serve with salad.

Treacle tart

4oz (100g) plain flour
2oz (50g) margarine
FILLING
8oz (225g) golden syrup

1 small lemon
1oz (25g) porridge oats
1½ oz (40g) breadcrumbs
1 egg

COST £

Make stale bread into breadcrumbs using a liquidiser or food processor and freeze in a plastic bag.

1 Preheat oven to 375°F, 190°C, Gas 5. Put flour and pinch of salt into a bowl. Add margarine, cut into pieces and rub in with fingertips until mixture resembles fine crumbs.

2 Stir in 4tsp water and mix to a smooth dough. Knead and roll out on a lightly floured surface.

Filling will harden slightly on cooling.

3 Lift pastry over a rolling pin and use to line a 7in (18.5cm) flan or sponge tin. Press pastry on to base and sides of tin and trim top.

4 Warm syrup in a saucepan. Grate lemon and squeeze juice. Stir into syrup with oats, breadcrumbs and beaten egg.

Freezes for up to 6 months.

5 Pour into tin and cook for 25–30 minutes until browned. Leave to cool then cut into wedges and serve warm.

Store cupboard ingredients.

SHOPPING LIST

FRUIT AND VEGETABLES

8 small onions
2lb (900g) potatoes
2 medium-sized baking potatoes
3 small parsnips
4 carrots
2 small leeks
6oz (150g) button mushrooms

8oz (225g) broccoli
12oz (325g) Brussels sprouts
5 tomatoes
1 red pepper
1 green pepper
2 courgettes
1 small head of celery

1 tub of mustard and cress
1 round lettuce
4 dessert apples
1 pear
1 lemon
2 bananas
2 oranges

DAIRY PRODUCE

8 eggs
2½ pt (1.5 litre) semi-skimmed milk

6oz (150g) Stilton
8oz (225g) tub cottage cheese

3oz (75g) Cheddar cheese
1lb 3½oz (540g) margarine

FRESH MEAT

2 chicken thighs
8oz (225g) pack of 4 bacon steaks

2oz (50g) black pudding
4oz (100g) thinly sliced smoked ham

1¼lb (550g) thick end belly pork

FROZEN FOODS

8oz (225g) tub chicken livers
1lb (450g) neck of (stewing) lamb

2 x 4oz (100g) cod steaks
3tbsp frozen chopped parsley

6 scoops vanilla ice cream
3oz (75g) frozen peas

BREAD

1 small white sliced loaf   1 small Granary loaf   2 pitta breads

CANS AND DRY GOODS

14oz (397g) can tomatoes

8oz (227g) can tomatoes

8oz (227g) can crushed pineapple

4oz (100g) continental green lentils

4tbsp mincemeat

14oz (400g) mixed dried fruit

4oz (100g) pasta shells or quills

4oz (100g) easy-cook brown rice

1lb 5oz (575g) self-raising flour

3oz (75g) suet

STORE CUPBOARD

5½ oz (140g) plain flour

4oz (100g) wholemeal flour

3oz (75g) porridge oats

4tbsp demerara sugar

7oz (200g) soft light brown sugar

1½ oz (40g) caster sugar

3oz (75g) granulated sugar

5tbsp marmalade

1½ oz (40g) sultanas

1tbsp flaked almonds, optional

2tbsp Parmesan

3 garlic cloves

2tsp Worcestershire sauce

2tsp tomato ketchup

2tbsp tomato purée

3tsp coarse grain mustard

¼pt (150ml) sunflower oil

2 chicken stock cubes

2 vegetable stock cubes

1 lamb stock cube

HERBS AND SPICES

½ tsp dried thyme

¼ tsp dried marjoram

¼ tsp dried rosemary

pinch paprika

½ tsp turmeric

½ tsp ground cinnamon

1 cinnamon stick

1tsp grated nutmeg

4 cloves

EXTRAS

1 large Mars bar

Pot roast pork with ratatouille

COST £££

It is cheaper to buy pork from the butchers. Ask for 'thick end of belly', it's much leaner.

If you don't have a casserole dish the right size — use a pie dish.

1 small onion

2 sticks celery

1 courgette

½ red pepper

1 garlic clove, crushed, optional

2 tbsp tomato purée

½ tsp dried thyme

1¼ lb (550g) thick end of belly pork

2 medium-sized baking potatoes

½ oz (15g) butter or margarine, optional

1 Preheat oven to 400°F, 200°C, Gas 6. Slice onion and celery. Halve courgette lengthways then slice. Cut pepper into strips, discarding core and any seeds.

2 Put all vegetables into the base of a casserole dish. Add garlic, tomato purée, thyme, 6tbsp water and seasoning. Mix together.

3 Score pork skin with a sharp knife if not already done by butcher. Sprinkle with salt and place pork on top of vegetables.

4 Prick potatoes and cook alongside pork on centre oven shelf for 1¼ hours until juices run clear when pork is pierced with a skewer and potatoes are tender.

5 Lift pork out of dish, cut away crackling and break into pieces. Carve meat into thin slices. Arrange on serving plates with ratatouille mixture and split jacket potatoes dotted with butter or margarine if using. Spoon ratatouille juices over pork.

■ If crackling doesn't crackle, cut off rind, sprinkle with salt and grill.

■ For good crackling, score pork with a new Stanley knife (much sharper than a kitchen knife) kept only for cooking! Rub salt well into skin and cook, uncovered.

Caramel oranges

2 oranges   3oz (75g) granulated sugar

1 Cut top and bottom off each orange with a serrated knife. Stand oranges on a chopping board then cut peel and pith away beginning at the top and cutting down towards base.

2 Hold each orange over a glass dish and cut away segments. Squeeze juice from membrane into dishes.

3 Put sugar into a small, heavy-based saucepan with 2tbsp water. Heat gently without stirring until completely dissolved. Increase heat and boil for 8–10 minutes, without stirring, until a pale golden colour.

4 Remove from heat, stand well back and add 1tbsp boiling water. (Syrup will spit as water is added.) Pour over oranges and chill until required.

COST £

Quick to make.

High in vitamin C.

Store cupboard ingredients.

Farmhouse fruit cake

COST ££

To test when a fruit cake is done, insert a skewer into centre. It will come out cleanly if cake is cooked.

Store cupboard ingredients.

5oz (125g) soft margarine
5oz (125g) light brown sugar
2 eggs
7oz (200g) self-raising flour
8oz (227g) can crushed pineapple
14oz (400g) mixed dried fruit

1 Preheat oven to 325°F, 160°C, Gas 3. Grease and line base and sides of a 7in (18.5cm) deep round tin with greaseproof paper and grease the paper.

2 Cream margarine and sugar together until light and fluffy. Beat eggs and gradually mix into margarine alternately with flour.

3 Drain pineapple and stir into cake mixture with dried fruit.

4 Spoon into tin and level surface. Cook in the centre of the oven for 1½ –1¾ hours.

5 Cool in tin then turn out and peel away paper. Cut into slices to serve.

■ **If you don't have the right size tin and use a larger one, the cake will cook quicker.**
■ **Cake will store in an airtight tin up to ten days.**

Brussels sprout and Stilton soup

I small onion	pinch grated nutmeg
I small potato	8fl oz (240ml)
8oz (225g) Brussels sprouts	semi-skimmed milk
1oz (25g) margarine	2oz (50g) Stilton cheese
¹/₂ pt (300ml) vegetable stock	

COST £ £

1 Chop onion, dice potato and quarter sprouts. Heat margarine in a saucepan and fry onion and potato for 5 minutes, stirring occasionally, until softened but not browned. Add sprouts and cook for 3 minutes.

2 Add stock, nutmeg and seasoning and bring to the boil. Stir well, cover, and simmer for 15 minutes until vegetables are tender.

3 Cool slightly then process or liquidise until smooth. Return to pan and stir in milk. Derind cheese, break into small pieces and add to soup.

4 Reheat, stirring occasionally, until cheese has melted. Ladle into bowls and serve with crusty bread.

For less fat, soup also tastes good without cheese.

Don't overcook or sprouts will lose their bright colour.

MONDAY SUPPER

Mustard chicken

COST £ £

High protein.

If you don't have a steamer, use a colander over a saucepan and cover with a large saucepan lid.

I small onion

2oz (50g) button mushrooms

I tbsp sunflower oil

2 chicken thighs

I tbsp plain flour

$^1/_2$ tsp turmeric

$^1/_2$ pt (300ml) chicken stock

2tsp coarse grain mustard

2 small parsnips

2 carrots

4oz (100g) broccoli

$^1/_2$ oz (15g) margarine

1 Preheat oven to 375° F, 190° C, Gas 5. Slice onion and mushrooms. Heat oil in a flameproof casserole and fry onion and chicken until lightly browned.

2 Add mushrooms and cook for 3 minutes. Add flour and turmeric and mix together.

3 Stir in stock, mustard and seasoning. Bring to the boil, cover and transfer to the oven. Cook on centre oven shelf for 40 minutes.

4 Meanwhile, dice parsnips and carrots. Cook in a saucepan of boiling, lightly salted water for 25 minutes. Cut broccoli into florets and steam above root vegetables for last 5 minutes.

5 Drain and mash root vegetables with margarine. Spoon on to serving plates with broccoli and chicken.

Marmalade bread and butter pudding

5 small slices bread	2tbsp sultanas
1oz (25g) butter or soft margarine	1 egg
2tbsp marmalade	7fl oz (210ml) semi-skimmed milk
2tbsp caster sugar	

COST £

Quick to make.

Store cupboard ingredients.

1 Spread bread with butter or margarine then marmalade. Cut each slice of bread into 4 triangles.

2 Lightly grease a 1pt (600ml) pie dish and arrange bread triangles in dish, sprinkling layers with sugar and sultanas.

3 Beat egg and milk together in a small bowl. Strain into dish.

4 Cook alongside Mustard chicken at 375°F, 190°C, Gas 5 for 30 minutes until golden brown and egg mixture has set. Serve warm.

Chicken liver pâté

COST £

High in iron.

For a special
occasion, add sherry
instead of stock.

Make night before
and chill in fridge, if
preferred.

1 small onion
8oz (225g) frozen
chicken livers, just thawed
1oz (25g) margarine
1 garlic clove, crushed
6tbsp chicken stock

TO SERVE
Granary toast
few lettuce leaves
2 sticks celery

1 Finely chop onion. Put chicken livers into a sieve and wash thoroughly with cold water. Drain and roughly chop, discarding any white parts.

2 Heat margarine in a frying pan, add onion and fry for 5 minutes, stirring occasionally until softened.

3 Add livers and garlic and fry over a high heat for 2 minutes, stirring until browned.

4 Add stock and seasoning and simmer for 5 minutes until livers are cooked and some of the liquid has evaporated.

5 Cool slightly then process or liquidise until smooth. Spoon into 2 small ramekins and chill for several hours until set. Serve with toast, lettuce and celery.

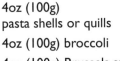

Saucy Stilton pasta

4oz (100g)
pasta shells or quills

4oz (100g) broccoli

4oz (100g) Brussels sprouts

1oz (25g) margarine

1oz (25g) plain flour

¹/₂ pt (300ml)
semi-skimmed milk

4oz (100g) Stilton cheese

1 tomato

1 Cook pasta in a saucepan of boiling, lightly salted water for 10 minutes until tender.

2 Meanwhile, cut broccoli into small florets and stalks into thick slices. Trim and quarter sprouts. Add to pasta pan for last 5 minutes of cooking.

3 Drain pasta and vegetables, rinse with boiling water and drain again.

4 Dry saucepan and melt margarine. Stir in flour and cook for 1 minute. Gradually add milk and bring to the boil, stirring until thickened and smooth.

5 Derind Stilton, roughly chop and stir into sauce with seasoning. Heat, stirring, until cheese has melted then stir in pasta and vegetables.

6 Spoon into serving dishes and garnish with sliced tomatoes. Serve immediately.

COST ££

Quick to make.

Could use Cheddar in place of Stilton, or add left-over strips of ham or grilled bacon.

Winter fruit compôte

COST £

Quick to make.

Cheaper to buy
cinnamon sticks loose
or in plastic packets.

Low calorie.

2 dessert apples
1 ripe pear
1 cinnamon stick
4 cloves
2tbsp demerara or
soft light brown sugar

1 Quarter, core and peel apples and pear. Cut into thick slices and put into a small saucepan.

2 Break cinnamon stick into 2 or 3 pieces and add to pan with cloves, sugar and 3fl oz (90ml) water.

3 Bring to the boil, cover and simmer for 5 minutes. Leave to cool so spice flavours can develop. Reheat to serve. Discard spices just before eating.

Spanish omelette

I medium potato	I tbsp sunflower oil
I small onion	3 eggs
¹/₄ red pepper	2 tbsp semi-skimmed milk
¹/₂ green pepper	2 tomatoes

1 Dice potato and cook in boiling, lightly salted water for 5 minutes until tender. Drain and set aside.

2 Finely chop onion. Dice peppers discarding core and any seeds.

3 Heat oil in an 8in (20cm) frying pan, add vegetables and fry for 5 minutes, stirring occasionally, until lightly browned.

4 Meanwhile, beat eggs, milk and seasoning together.

5 Add eggs to pan and cook, without stirring, until underside is golden brown and eggs are almost set. Transfer to the grill and cook until eggs are set.

6 Cut into large wedges and transfer to serving plates. Serve with sliced tomatoes.

COST £

Quick to make.

High protein.

Vary the ingredients — 2 chopped rashers streaky bacon, diced courgette, few sliced mushrooms — according to stores.

Leek and bacon pie

COST £££

Use pre-packed bacon steaks rather than gammon steaks as they're cheaper.

Could use shortcrust or bought puff pastry.

8oz (225g)
pack of 4 bacon steaks

2 small leeks

1oz (25g) margarine

1oz (25g) plain flour

¹/₂ pt (300ml)
semi-skimmed milk

2tbsp frozen
chopped parsley, optional

PASTRY

6oz (150g) self-raising flour

3oz (75g) suet

beaten egg or milk to glaze

TO SERVE

3oz (75g) frozen peas

1 Preheat the oven to 400°F, 200°C, Gas 6. Grill bacon steaks for 6 minutes, turning once. Cut into large dice.

2 Thoroughly wash leeks and slice thickly. Cook in boiling water for 2 minutes. Drain, rinse with cold water and drain again.

3 Melt margarine in dried pan. Stir in flour, cook for 1 minute. Gradually add milk and bring to the boil, stirring until thickened and smooth.

4 Stir in parsley, if using, bacon, leeks and seasoning. Spoon into a 1pt (600ml) pie dish.

5 Make pastry, put flour, suet and seasoning into a bowl. Add 7–8tbsp water and mix to a soft but not sticky dough.

6 Knead and roll out on a lightly floured surface until a little larger than top of pie dish.

7 Dampen edge of pie dish, cut a strip of pastry and press on to dish edge. Brush with water and place remaining pastry over pie. Press edges together to seal well and trim.

8 Knock up pastry edge with the back of a knife and crimp between fingers and thumb. Reroll pastry trimmings and cut out leaves. Place on pie and brush with egg or milk.

9 Cook for 30 minutes until pastry is well risen and golden. Cook peas in a saucepan of boiling, lightly salted water for last 5 minutes of pie cooking. Drain and serve with the pie.

■ **If your pie dish is too big, add a pastry funnel to support pastry in centre of pie.**

Ice cream and Mars bar sauce

1 large Mars bar
3 tbsp semi-skimmed milk
4 small scoops of vanilla ice cream

1 tbsp toasted flaked almonds, optional

COST £

1 Slice Mars bar and put into a small bowl set over a saucepan of simmering water. Add milk and heat gently until Mars bar has melted. Stir sauce.

Quick to make.

2 Arrange scoops of ice cream in two glass dishes. Spoon sauce over. Sprinkle with almonds if liked and serve at once.

Can microwave sauce, on Full Power (100%) for 1½ minutes.

Could also add sliced bananas.

THURSDAY LUNCH

Pitta pockets

COST ££

8oz (225g) tub plain cottage cheese

I tub mustard and cress

2 pitta breads

Low-calorie.

I Put cottage cheese and plenty of seasoning into a bowl. Snip mustard and cress leaves into cheese and mix together.

2 Sprinkle pitta breads with water and grill until puffy. Cut in half crossways and slit open into pockets with a small knife. Spoon in filling and serve immediately.

THURSDAY SUPPER

Lamb hotpot

COST ££

Buy black pudding from the deli counter; they'll cut just the amount you need.

Ilb (450g) frozen neck of (stewing) lamb, defrosted

I small onion

I small parsnip

I carrot

Itbsp sunflower oil

Itbsp plain flour

$1/2$ pt (300ml) lamb or chicken stock

$1/4$ tsp dried rosemary

2oz (50g) black pudding, optional

12oz (325g) potatoes

$1/2$oz (15g) margarine

I Preheat oven to 325°F, 160°C, Gas 3. Trim any fat from lamb. Finely chop onion. Dice parsnip and carrot.

2 Heat oil in a flameproof casserole, add lamb and onions and cook until lamb is browned on both sides.

3 Add parsnip and carrot and cook for 3 minutes more. Add flour and mix together.

4 Pour over stock, add rosemary and seasoning and bring to the boil.

5 Peel and dice black pudding, if using and add to casserole.

Could use a slow cooker, following manufacturer's directions.

6 Remove casserole from the heat. Slice potatoes and arrange overlapping over top of lamb and vegetables. Season and dot with margarine.

7 Cook uncovered for $1^{1}/_{2}$ hours until potatoes are lightly browned. Spoon into soup bowls to serve.

If potatoes are a little pale at end of cooking, brown under the grill.

PUDDING THURSDAY

Crêpes with marmalade sauce

2oz (50g) plain flour

1oz (25g) caster sugar

1 egg

2tbsp sunflower oil plus oil for frying

4fl oz (120ml) semi-skimmed milk and water mixed

3tbsp marmalade

COST £

Store cupboard ingredients.

1 Put flour, sugar and egg in a bowl and mix together. Gradually whisk in milk and water and 1tbsp oil until a smooth batter is formed.

2 Put marmalade in a small saucepan with 2tbsp water. Bring to the boil, stirring, until marmalade has melted then boil for a few minutes until syrupy. Set aside.

Aim to make the crêpes as thin as possible.

3 Pour a little oil into the base of a small non-stick frying pan. When hot, pour away excess oil. Add 2tbsp crêpe mixture, tilt pan until base is completely covered. Cook for a minute or two until base is lightly browned.

4 Turn crêpe over with a knife and cook the other side. Slide out of pan and keep crêpe hot. Repeat until all batter is used up.

5 Reheat sauce. Arrange crêpes on serving plates and spoon sauce over. Serve immediately.

Devilled mushrooms

4oz (100g) button mushrooms
1oz (25g) margarine
2tsp tomato ketchup

2tsp Worcestershire sauce
1tsp coarse grain mustard
2 slices buttered

COST £

Quick to make.

1 Slice mushrooms. Heat margarine in a frying pan, add mushrooms and fry for 3–4 minutes, stirring.

2 Add ketchup, Worcestershire sauce, mustard and seasoning and cook for 2 minutes, stirring.

3 Spoon on to buttered toast and serve immediately.

Fish creole

4oz (100g) easy-cook brown rice
1 small onion
1/2 green pepper
1/4 red pepper
1tbsp sunflower oil
2 x 4oz (100g) frozen cod pieces

1 small lemon, grated rind only (reserve lemon for Lentil moussaka)
8oz (227g) can tomatoes
1/4 tsp sugar
1/4 tsp dried marjoram
1 courgette

COST £££

High protein.

1 Cook rice in a saucepan of boiling, lightly salted water for 25 minutes until tender. Drain.

2 Meanwhile, thinly slice onion and cut peppers into thin strips, discarding any core and seeds.

Buy frozen fish, it's cheaper than fresh.

3 Heat oil in a frying pan, add onions and fry for 5 minutes until softened. Add peppers, fish, lemon rind, tomatoes, sugar, marjoram and seasoning, mix together.

4 Cover and simmer for 20 minutes until fish is cooked.

No need to thaw fish before cooking.

5 Slice courgette and steam above rice for last 5 minutes of cooking.

6 Arrange rice, fish and courgettes on serving plates and serve immediately.

■ **You can tell when fish is cooked – it flakes when pressed with a knife.**

FRIDAY PUDDING

Sticky bananas

COST £

Quick to make.

Store cupboard ingredients.

2 bananas
1oz (25g) margarine
1oz (25g) sultanas
1/2 orange, grated rind only

2tbsp demerara sugar or soft light brown sugar
2 scoops
vanilla ice cream, optional

1 Slice bananas. Heat margarine in a frying pan. Add bananas, sugar, orange rind and sultanas, and fry, stirring, for 3–4 minutes until bananas are hot through.

2 Spoon into serving dishes and serve with vanilla ice cream, if liked.

Cheese scones

3oz (75g) Cheddar cheese

8oz (225g) self-raising flour

2oz (50g) margarine

1 egg

1tsp coarse grain mustard

4tbsp semi-skimmed milk

pinch paprika

TO SERVE

butter or margarine for spreading

4oz (100g) thinly sliced smoked ham, optional

2 tomatoes

COST ££

Quick to make

Reheat scones individually in microwave, on Full Power (100%) for 20–30 seconds.

Freeze any leftovers in a plastic bag for up to 6 months.

Store cupboard ingredients.

1 Preheat oven to 425°F, 220°C, Gas 7. Grate cheese.

2 Put flour and seasoning into a bowl. Add margarine, cut into pieces and rub in with fingertips or an electric mixer until mixture resembles fine crumbs.

3 Beat egg in a cup, stir half into flour mixture with three-quarters of the cheese and the mustard and milk. Mix together to form a smooth dough.

4 Knead and roll out on a lightly floured surface until the size of a tea plate.

5 Transfer to a lightly greased baking sheet. Mark into 6 wedges and pull each slightly apart. Brush with remaining egg and sprinkle with remaining cheese. Sprinkle with a little paprika.

6 Cook for 20 minutes until well risen and golden brown. Serve warm, split and buttered or spread with margarine. Arrange on serving plates with ham and quartered tomatoes.

Lentil moussaka

COST £ £

High fibre.

Can be made earlier in the day. Reheat thoroughly when ready. Dress salad at last minute.

Can use bottled lemon juice.

Store cupboard ingredients.

I small onion
I carrot
2 sticks celery
I tbsp sunflower oil
I garlic clove, crushed
4oz (100g) continental green lentils
14oz (397g) can tomatoes
¼ pt (150ml) vegetable stock
½ tsp ground cinnamon
pinch grated nutmeg

TOPPING

Ilb (450g) potatoes
Ioz (25g) margarine
Ioz (25g) plain flour
½ pt (300ml) semi-skimmed milk
pinch grated nutmeg
2tbsp grated Parmesan or Cheddar cheese

TO SERVE

Itbsp sunflower oil
Itsp lemon juice (lemon reserved from Fish creole)
Itbsp frozen chopped parsley, optional
½ round lettuce

I Slice onion. Dice carrot and celery. Heat oil in a saucepan and fry vegetables for 5 minutes, stirring occasionally, until soft.

2 Add garlic, lentils, tomatoes, stock, spices and seasoning. Bring to the boil, stirring. Cover and simmer for 50 minutes, stirring occasionally and adding a little more stock towards end of cooking if needed.

3 Meanwhile, slice potatoes. Cook in a separate saucepan of boiling, lightly salted water for 4–5 minutes until just tender. Drain, rinse with cold water and drain again.

4 Dry pan. Heat margarine. Stir in flour and cook for 1 minute. Gradually add milk and bring to boil, stirring until thickened and smooth. Stir in nutmeg and seasoning.

5 Preheat oven to 400°F, 200°C, Gas 6. Spoon lentil mixture evenly into a shallow ovenproof dish. Arrange potatoes overlapping on top. Pour sauce over and sprinkle with cheese.

6 Cook moussaka on shelf just above centre of oven for 30 minutes until golden brown.

7 Meanwhile, make salad. Mix oil, lemon juice, parsley if using, and seasoning together in base of salad bowl. Wash and tear lettuce into bite-sized pieces. Add to dressing and toss together. Serve with Lentil moussaka.

■ **Dressing can be in base of bowl, with salad ready on top, but toss only at last minute.**

PUDDING SATURDAY

Mincemeat and apple crumble squares

3oz (75g) margarine	3oz (75g) porridge oats
2oz (50g) soft light brown sugar	4tbsp mincemeat
4oz (100g) wholemeal flour	2 dessert apples

COST ££

A good way to use up remaining Christmas mincemeat.

1 Melt margarine and sugar in a saucepan. Stir in flour and oats and mix together.

2 Press two-thirds of the oat mixture into the base of a lightly greased 7in (18.5cm) shallow square tin.

3 Spoon mincemeat on top and spread roughly with a knife. Quarter, core and peel apples. Slice and arrange in rows over the mincemeat.

Freeze any left-over squares individually wrapped in cling film so you can defrost as many as you need.

4 Sprinkle remaining oat mixture over and cook at 400°F, 200°C, Gas 6 on shelf just below Lentil moussaka for 30 minutes. Cut into squares and serve warm.

About Age Concern

Eating Well on a Budget is one of a wide range of publications produced by Age Concern England – National Council on Ageing. In addition, Age Concern is actively engaged in training, information provision, research and campaigning for retired people and those who work with them. It is a registered charity dependent on public support for the continuation of its work.

Age Concern England links closely with Age Concern centres in Scotland, Wales and Northern Ireland to form a network of over 1,400 independent local UK groups. These groups, with the invaluable help of an estimated 250,000 volunteers, aim to improve the quality of life for older people and develop services appropriate to local needs and resources. These include advice and information, day care, visiting services, transport schemes, clubs, and specialist facilities for physically and mentally frail older people.

Age Concern England
1268 London Road
London SW16 4ER
Tel: 081-679 8000

Age Concern Wales
4th Floor
1 Cathedral Road
Cardiff CF1 9SD
Tel: 0222 371566

Age Concern Scotland
54a Fountainbridge
Edinburgh EH3 9PT
Tel: 031-228 5656

Age Concern Northern Ireland
3 Lower Crescent
Belfast BT7 1NR
Tel: 0232 245729

Publications from ◆A◆C◆E◆ Books

A wide range of titles is published by Age Concern England under the ACE Books imprint.

MONEY MATTERS
Your Taxes and Savings
Jennie Hawthorne and Sally West
Explains how the tax system affects people over retirement age, including how to avoid paying more tax than necessary. The information about savings covers the wide range of investment opportunities now available.
Further information on application.

Your Rights
Sally West
A highly acclaimed annual guide to the State benefits available to older people. Contains current information on Income Support, Housing Benefit and Retirement Pensions, among other matters, and includes advice on how to claim them.
Further information on application.

Managing Other People's Money
Penny Letts
The management of money and property is usually a personal and private matter. However, there may come a time when someone else has to take over on either a temporary or permanent basis. This book

looks at the circumstances in which such a need could arise and provides a step-by-step guide to the arrangements which have to be made.
£5.95 0-86242-090-3

HOUSING

Housing Options for Older People
David Bookbinder

A review of housing options is part of growing older. All the possibilities and their practical implications are carefully considered in this comprehensive guide.
£4.95 0–86242–108–X

An Owner's Guide: Your Home in Retirement

This definitive guide considers all aspects of home maintenance of concern to retired people and those preparing for retirement, providing advice on heating, insulation and home security. Co-published with the National Housing and Town Planning Council.
£2.50 0–86242–095–4

GENERAL

Living, Loving and Ageing: Sexual and personal relationships in later life
Wendy Greengross and Sally Greengross

Sexuality is often regarded as the preserve of the younger generation. At last, here is a book for older people, and those who work with them, which tackles the issues in a straightforward fashion, avoiding preconceptions and bias.
£4.95 0–86242–070–9

Looking Good, Feeling Good
Nancy Tuft

Positive, upbeat and awash with useful advice and ideas, this book encourages the over 50s to take pride in their appearance and challenges the popular view that interest in fashion and beauty passes with the years. Illustrated in full colour.
£7.95 0–86242–102–0

An Active Retirement
Nancy Tuft

Bursting with information on hobbies, sports, educational opportunities and voluntary work, this practical guide is ideal for retired people seeking new ways to fill their time but uncertain where to start.

£7.95   0–86242–119–5

HEALTH
In Control: Help with incontinence
Penny Mares

Containing information about the nature and causes of incontinence and the sources of help available, this book has been written for anyone concerned about this problem, either professionally or at home. The text is illustrated throughout with drawings and case histories.

£4.50   0–86242–088–1

Know Your Medicines
Pat Blair

We would all like to know more about the medicines we take. The second edition of this successful guide is written for older people and their carers and examines how the body works and the effects of medication.

£6.50   0–86242–100–4

To order books, please send a cheque or money order to the address below. Postage and packing are free. Credit card orders may be made on 081-679 8000.

Age Concern England (DEPT EW)
PO Box 9
London
SW16 4EX

Information factsheets

Age Concern England produces over 30 factsheets on a variety of subjects, and among these the following titles may be of interest to readers of this book:

Factsheet 1   *Help with Heating*
Factsheet 12 *Raising Income or Capital from Your Home*
Factsheet 15 *Income Tax and Older People*
Factsheet 18 *A Brief Guide to Money Benefits*
Factsheet 26 *Travel Information for Older People*

To order factsheets
Single copies are free on receipt of a 9" x 6" sae. If you require a selection of factsheets or multiple copies totalling more than 10, charges will be given on request.

A complete set of factsheets is available in a ring binder at the current cost of £32, which includes the first year's subscription. The current cost for annual subscription for subsequent years is £12. There are different rates of subscription for people living abroad.

Factsheets are revised and updated throughout the year and membership of the subscription service will ensure that your information is always current.

> For further information, or to order factsheets, write to:
> **Information and Policy Department**
> Age Concern England
> 1268 London Road
> London SW16 4ER

About the sponsor

The Unigate group has grown out of three of England's oldest dairy companies, Aplin & Barrett, Wilts United Dairies and Cow & Gate.

Early in the century Aplin & Barrett started making St Ivel Lactic cheese, the first nationally advertised dairy product, and the name 'St Ivel' still graces many of Unigate's Fresh Foods today.

Unigate Dairies, the milk division of Unigate, plays an important part in the operation that collects milk from the farms, puts it into bottles or turns it into butter, cream and cheese before delivering it to your doorstep or to shops and restaurants. Unigate Dairies gave our industry the Care Code from which you may have benefited personally.

This Care Code that every milkman and woman operates was devised back in the late 1960's by United Dairies. In 1971, it was adopted by the whole British doorstep delivery industry.

It really only put into words what the people who put milk and other goods on the doorstep have been doing for years – looking out for signs that people on their rounds are not safe and well, and calling the emergency services if necessary.

In the early hours when few other people are about, they have prevented fires spreading to cause danger, summoned help for old people lying helpless after a fall, and even 'blown the whistle' on a few criminals.

The people on the rounds are a warm-hearted lot, and so their caring goes further.

One of our Unigate Dairies milkmen ran raffles, raised sponsorship and enlisted the aid of suppliers and a taxi firm to give a Christmas lunch for all the old people on his round who would be spending the holiday alone.

Others change bulbs, run errands, post letters, and start cars on cold mornings. One lady who is a Unigate Dairies customer never fills her car with petrol. She is nervous of petrol, so her milkman takes it down to the garage and fills it up for her.

Milkmen and women offer a patient hand of friendship – even though everyone wants their milk before eight o'clock in the morning.

In addition to all the other talents they need to do the job properly, they have had to become a sort of 'mobile shopkeeper' as well.

Britain's doorstep delivery service is highly prized – companies like Unigate Dairies and their staff are determined to maintain the service.

Not everyone can get to the supermarket. Even the local shop may be an inconvenient distance away. And who would pop in for a friendly chat with someone on their own? Who else would notice a stranger wandering round the house when the family is away?

It's a worthwhile service to keep, and to do it your milkman and woman must serve more than a pint of milk. Butter, eggs and potatoes; bread, tea and plastic sacks are on their shopping list for customers nowadays. Strawberries and cream (especially in Wimbledon fortnight). Christmas puddings in the hampers for which their customers buy savings stamps throughout the year.

The first doorstep deliveries were by milkmaids with two buckets of milk hanging from the wooden yoke on their shoulders.

Today's milk float is just as quiet with its environmentally-friendly electric motor, but it is packed with a range of goods the milkmaid could never have managed. Bottling, packaging and cool boxes are also designed to provide standards of hygiene immensely higher than an open bucket, so that when you eat and drink Unigate you do it in the healthiest and most convenient way.

Index to the recipes